MW01001253

THE LOONEY EXPERIMENT

BY LUKE REYNOLDS

BLINK

ONE

THUNDER, THE SILVER-HAIRED MAN, AND THE USUAL RESULTS

"Atticus, we really don't have all day. Would you please move a little faster?" Mrs. Kathan looks at me and rubs her belly. It's a big belly. The kind of belly a marble would roll right off if placed anywhere on it. Even if the marble didn't roll off, the baby inside would probably kick it off.

"*Atticus!* Can you hear me?"

"Yes, Mrs. Kathan. Yes, I mean, I can, um, yes . . ." The words feel like wet sand in my mouth.

"Get up and give your speech, Atticus. *Now.*" Mrs. Kathan's chair squeaks as she leans back. I know she's not trying to be mean, and all through the winter and spring she's told us that having a baby in your belly makes you more emotional than normal. Okay. Fine. But I'm already terrified, and listening to someone "more emotional" tell me to hurry up isn't helping any.

I don't know why I can't speak in class. All I know is that when I try to get what's in my head to come out for other people to hear, it doesn't work.

It never works.

I pretend to shuffle my papers some more. I put my index cards with their big ROBERT FROST lettering into my red folder. Then I unclip the red folder from my three-ring binder. Then I take the index cards back out, clip my red folder back into my binder, flip my binder closed, and—

"*Atticus!* Get up there now, or you're getting an F on the poet report and your mom will get another call from me. We have seven more students who need to give their reports today and I—*ah, ooh*—I am not going to put up with this hemming and hawing garbage again. Do you hear me?" Mrs. Kathan leans way to the left in her chair, grabs her belly-with-the-baby-inside, and shimmies around. Her face stretches out like she's about to blow painful bubbles.

I stand up and start walking toward the podium.

Danny, Audrey, *everyone.* They're all there. Watching me. Waiting for what they know and I know and everybody knows is going to happen. So I have no choice. It starts banging on the doors of my head and I decide to just let it in, let it take over.

My Imagination.

Robert Frost, the poet himself, suddenly opens the door to our English classroom and strolls in, like we've all been waiting for him anyway, and like he had promised me he was going to come. Looking at me, his eyes wrinkle up, and then he shoots me this wise look. Beneath his silver hair, his face rises up like a wave about to crash. Then his voice booms like the room is too small for it. "Atticus, my friend! I heard about this report you were giving on me, and I wanted to be here as well! You are a delightful young man, and I'm sure you'll teach even me about myself!"

And I look at Robert Frost and reply, with a smile and a laugh, "Hi, Robert! Nice to see you again! I'm psyched you could make it in for my speech. This is Mrs. Kathan, my English teacher . . ." And then Mrs. Kathan blushes like Christmas. She's feeling so bad about the way she just talked to me. Even the baby inside her belly is thinking, *Jeez, Mom, give the kid a break, will you?!*

Then Robert Frost kind of glides over to me like he's on roller skates, and he throws his arm around me. He winks at me and says, "The floor is yours, Son." Just like that, he calls me *Son* and nods his head like we know something secret between the two of us and we're about to let the whole world in on it.

Together, Robert Frost and I walk up to the podium, where we recite some of his poetry back and forth, each of us saying a stanza. Just as soon as one of us stops reciting, the other one picks up like we're having a baseball catch—just tossing these lines of poetry back and forth, and it all feels so good, and we keep catching the lines and neither of us is afraid of dropping the ball. Because we don't, and we can't.

I sense her eyes, so I glance toward the room after I toss the lines back to Robert Frost, and I'm right: Audrey Higgins is looking at me like *Atticus, you are amazing, incredible, so confident and brave and smart and poetic and—*

And I am not afraid.

And my voice is like thunder.

Like thunder!

Two roads diverged in a yellow wood. The lines of Robert Frost leap from my mouth.

The *Thundering* Atticus!

The *Brave* Atticus!

The *Bold* Atticus!

Not the Terrified—

"*ATTICUS!* You open your mouth, and you speak. That's it. I'm going to treat you like my five-year-old son; I'm going to count to ten, and if you don't start your report before I get to ten, you can sit down and you will get an F. Then Margaret is up." Mrs. Kathan looks at me with eyes like the points of nails.

I tell my Imagination to *shut up*. I stand in front of the podium and open my mouth. "Two roads . . ." I clear my throat. "I mean, two roads," I try to force the wet sand out of my voice.

But my voice refuses.

"Two roads diverged in a—"

"Fatticus, I can't hear you! Can you please *speak up!*" Danny Wills cups his hands together as he launches the words toward me.

"Danny, *I'll* be the one to tell Atticus what to do, all right? You just sit there until I tell you to speak! And what did you call him?" Mrs. Kathan has swiveled around in her rolling chair to face Danny at the back of the class. He wears a smirk and a baseball cap. We weren't allowed to wear hats in school until Danny's mom got herself elected to the school board, and now students can wear any kind of hat they want in school.

The smirk grows like bacteria across Danny's face, threatening to take over all the skin that remains.

"I called him *Atticus*, Mrs. Kathan. Isn't that his name?" Danny tips back in his chair, and the bacteria finally does it. Bam! It surrounds his face, and the skin is gone and the smirk is wild, free.

I let it happen again with my Imagination. I can't help it. (And maybe I don't want to.)

Robert Frost goes over to Danny and pulls the chair backward so that Danny falls and smacks his head on the floor. Then Robert Frost says, "Whoops. Did I do that?" Robert Frost looks up at me and gives me another nod, another wink, then a thumbs-up with his right hand for good measure, and I let my head lean backward and laugh so loud it hurts. It hurts so much but I can't stop laughing because Robert Frost is laughing too, and it doesn't help you stop laughing when you're *trying* to stop laughing but probably the best poet of all time just keeps on laughing like he's inviting you to laugh because you know it's all going to be completely—

"Fine! Danny, Put . . . your . . . chair . . . down . . . *now!*" Mrs. Kathan grabs her belly as if the baby is going to pop out right here in the middle of fourth period.

Meanwhile, I snap out of my Imagination and catch Audrey's eyes. The girl is the Fourth of July, my birthday, and Christmas all put together. I have loved Audrey Higgins for as long as I can remember, and she's been nice to me—you know, helping me pick up my binders after Danny knocks them down in the hallway or smiling at me to let me know that she knows that YES, I EXIST!

Right now, she's telling me something silently. Her mouth is moving, at least, and she's looking *right at me*, so she must be telling me something, right?

"Ugh! Why do I even try?" Mrs. Kathan turns back to face me again. "Okay, Atticus, here we go. One, two, three, four . . ." She's counting fast. She's counting like lightning.

Audrey does it again—the silent-words thing. *You . . .* something else, something else, something else . . .

My Imagination keeps kicking in too—Robert Frost keeps yelling out, "Your turn, Son! Your turn to recite a stanza! Go for it, Son! Tossing the lines to you . . . catch!"

"Five, six, seven . . ." Mrs. Kathan's numbers are flashes. *You . . . can . . .* Audrey stares hard at me.

"My son! Why, did you not hear me? I said, it's your turn to recite a stanza. Come on, now, just let your voice out of its cage, Son!"

"Eight, nine . . ." Mrs. Kathan continues. *You can do it,* Audrey mouths.

"Son!"

"Ten," Mrs. Kathan says in a voice as flat as a paved road. Audrey Higgins looks like she could cry.

Robert Frost lowers his head and then shakes it from side to side; he won't look me in the face anymore.

Mrs. Kathan puts her hands up to her face and rubs her eyes. "I just don't get it, Atticus. All you have to do is say the words on your index cards. I just—*ah*—don't get it."

As I take my seat, I feel something hard spike the back of my head. When I turn around to look, I see the smirk on Danny's face.

"*Fatticus*," he whispers.

This is what life is like for me, the kid with no guts and the World's Worst Name: Atticus.

STRIKING OUT

When I get home from school, Adrian is watching *The Never-Ending Story* for the 122nd time. I'm not kidding. My six-year-old brother has watched that DVD just about every day after school since my mom got it for him this past Christmas. She said it was one of her all-time favorite movies and that he probably hadn't ever heard of it because it was twenty years old or something.

As I walk through the living room, giving Adrian a pop on the head, he yells to me, "Atticus, the Rock Giant is about to come on. Watch it with me!"

"Adrian, look, I know that the Rock Giant is going to die, and everyone's going to be all *boo-hoo* and everything, and that in the end the white-haired dragon will come and make everything fine. I don't need to watch it again, okay?"

"Come on, Atticus, *please*?" But I'm not in the mood after what happened in English class today. Plus, I have to get ready for a baseball game.

I leave him on the couch and start up the stairs fast. That's where my mom catches me.

"Hey, honey, why so mean to Adrian?" She puts her hand on the right side of my face, and I feel something in me relax a little bit. I know it's not at all cool (and I know if someone like Danny *ever* knew this about me, he'd make my life even more miserable), but when my mom touches my face like that, everything calms down.

"It just wasn't great at school again, okay?" I try not to look at her.

"Why not?" She seems so calm, even though I know she and my dad have been screaming A LOT at night when they think Adrian and I are both asleep upstairs.

"It's just that I *hate* English class, and I don't ever want to go back there again." As I say the words, I finally look at my mom. Her eyes are closed, and she brings her hand up to her face like she's going to cry. So then I look past her at the monstrous pictures framed and hanging along the stairwell. There are pictures of me when I was a baby, when I was two, four, and on and on. Adrian too. I always look so happy in those pictures.

"But you used to love English. Remember how much you wrote, and how you read all the books before you even had to?" My mom combs my hair with her fingers.

Before I can explain, I hear the front door open and shut. Then my dad's voice comes up loud to meet me. "You ready or what? Game starts in thirty minutes. Let's go."

My mom looks down at the steps and lets her hands drop to her side.

I leave my mom in the stairwell and run up to put on my ridiculous baseball uniform. It's bright red with a picture of a tiger eating a fish. I'm serious. The tiger's fangs are ripping the head off of the fish, and blood is spurting out of the thing. Across this design, the words read: THE TOUGH TIGERS.

I hate the shirt. But Danny designed it, and Danny's father (whose name is *actually* Bill Wills) said the design "demonstrates what a real baseball team is all about." I wish I could play for a fake baseball team, then, because the design seriously stinks.

I throw the shirt on, ditch my school jeans, and start to put on the really stupid gray tights they make us wear in this Babe Ruth league. As I'm pulling the tights up, my Imagination grumbles, kicks in, and before I know it Gray Tights is moving, he has a voice, he's hearing my thoughts as if I'm shouting the words aloud—

Me: *Man, these STUPID, STUPID, STUPID gray tights. Whoever invented these tights, anyway? What genius one day sat down in his living room and decided,* Aha! I've got it! Boys who play baseball will wear tight gray pants that feel itchy and ridiculous!

Gray Tights: *Hey, Atticus, why are you attacking me? I mean, for real? I was made in the factory, and I sat in the store for a while, and then your dad brought me home to you. All I ever asked for was someone to love me. That's all I've ever wanted.*

Me: *If you and all the other Gray Tights in the factory refused to leave, refused to go out and do what everyone was telling you to do, then you would have saved countless people from a mountain of humiliation—*

Gray Tights: *Refuse to exist?! Are you crazy? This is the only life I've got, buddy, and I don't want to lose it. Plus, can you imagine refusing that kind of power? I mean, really, can you even do that?*

I hear a knock on my door, and I realize suddenly that I'm sitting on the edge of my bed, no pants on, with Gray Tights just below my knees.

"Let's go, Atticus. We're going to be late." My dad's voice sounds more hollow than normal.

"Yeah, I know," I say, pulling up the dreaded, *actual* gray tights of doom.

ⓖ ⓞ ⓖ

At Levy Field, I mainly sit the bench. Like usual. Coach Wills knows I stink. Danny knows I stink. I know I stink. The whole team knows I stink. The only reason I even come to the games is because it's the only thing my dad wants to do with me.

I don't play in the field, but league rules say that everyone on the team has to bat. Today, I strike out in all three of my at bats. Each time, as I drag myself back to my spot on the bench, Danny whispers, *Fatticus,* and then laughs like it's the most brilliant thing ever. But hey, what's so brilliant about putting an F in front of my name? So I'm fat. Fine. So I've got to wear stupid glasses. Fine. So I've got curly hair that makes me look like I have the biggest roller coaster *ever* right on top of my head. Fine. But what about Danny? The way he acts, I wish I had the courage to put an F in front of *his* name and roar out, *Fanny!*

In the ninth inning, our team is down by one, 3–2. We have two outs and one man on second base. I'm due up at the plate.

Coach Wills stops the game and goes out onto the field to talk with the umpire—a guy who looks like he could actually eat me for dinner with a side of potatoes. They talk for a while, laugh for a while, then frown for a while. Finally, Coach Wills comes back to the dugout shaking his head and rubbing his chin.

Danny asks him, "What's wrong, Dad?"

"Ump said Atticus has to bat, unless he's injured." Then Coach looks at me and shrugs. I grab my helmet and bat and trudge out to the mound, ignoring the stinging in my eyes and the tickle in my throat as best as I can.

Behind me, I overhear Danny say to his father, "I could injure him if that would help." And then a bunch of chuckles from the rest of the team.

At the plate, I stand way outside the batter's box.

"Come on now, kid, you know you've got to be inside the box for the pitches to count, right?" The ump removes his facemask and gives me this look, like he's wondering if he's going to put ketchup on me as well as the potatoes, or just some salt, before he devours me.

"Yes, um, yeah." I feel the words come out in a whisper. I don't know why I'm afraid of my words, but I sure as heck know why I'm afraid of the pitcher's fastball. That thing could knock my head off. Which would make the ump happier than all heaven because then he'd have my head right there, like it was served up for him.

I step just inside the batter's box, and the pitcher reams one right past me. I don't even see the thing, but I hear a *wppt* as it lands in the catcher's glove.

"Steeerike one!" the ump calls as he jabs his right hand in the air like he's practicing dragon slaying. All I can think is: *I wish it took just two strikes to get out.*

Up in the bleachers I see my mom, dad, and Adrian. My dad's fist is closed tightly, raised in the air, and he's gritting his teeth. My mom is smiling. Adrian is in between them playing with something.

The second pitch comes just as fast as the first, but this time I try to send the bat around the plate. I feel my swing still swooshing over home when the sound of the ball in the catcher's glove slaps my ears.

"Steeerike two!" And again, the dragon-slaying maneuver.

In our dugout, Coach Wills and my teammates are already packing up the equipment.

And that's when my Imagination takes over. All of a sudden, there is an announcer's voice in my head—it's low, and it's smooth, but it's also incredibly excited . . .

Here at Levy Field today, we've got a packed stadium, ladies and gents. Atticus Hobart at the plate, with the Tough

Tigers trailing by one. This at-bat could literally be a game changer, and we sure don't see teams this close with these Tigers very often. With an undefeated record, this could be quite the blemish on Coach Wills' perfect season.

And Hobart steps into the batter's box. Look at his eyes, folks! Talk about a Tough Tiger! Hobart is the very image of one right now. The pitcher nods at the call . . . the wind up . . . the pitch . . . HOLY COW! Hobart has come around with a ferocious swing, and that ball is on its way to the moon. It is up, way up, way, WAY UP . . . and going, going, GONE! Hobart has done it for the Tigers!

It's not until I hear the ump's grunting voice that I realize the dragon is dead, and dinner is served.

My dad and mom don't say a word the whole ride home. I keep thinking that it's because of me, that I've failed my dad too many times. If I could just get one single, stupid hit, then he would be happy. He'd be proud of me. And he'd say so.

Instead, the entire trip, the only sounds in the car are from Adrian, making farting noises and saying, "No, check out this one, this one is going to be the *best!*"

As soon as we get back in the house, my mom says, "All right, James, this is what you want. You tell Atticus yourself. I'm taking Adrian out of here. He's not going to find out like this."

Then my dad says, "Helen, don't make me out to be the bad guy here. You heard what the therapist said—I need more freedom to find out who I really am. That's all this is—some time to *explore* myself."

My mom grunts then—well, maybe it is more of a grunt-screechy thing. It begins like a grunt, but then her voice gets really high and really loud, and then she grabs Adrian, turns around, and leaves.

My dad comes over to me and says, "Sport, we've got some things to talk about."

I sense that something terrible is coming. But I don't look at my dad, and my Imagination threatens to wake up Gray Tights. But my dad takes my silence in stride and keeps what's real right in front of me.

"Okay, there is just no easy way to say this. I've got to leave for a while. I mean, leave you and your mother and Adrian—just for *a while*. I need to . . . I need to figure some things out, and I just can't do that here."

He pauses, looks away from me and at the bookshelf, and then back at me.

My dad is a pudgy guy with a bushy mustache and a few freckles scattered on the bottom of his chin. When I was a kid, I remember that he used to tickle me on my belly with his mustache, and I'd just about die laughing. Now, I want to rip the thing off his face, blend it into his morning coffee, and watch him drink the whole mess.

"Fine, just get out of here then." My mouth stammers out the words quietly, even though I want to roar them.

My dad doesn't say another word; he doesn't even try to hug me good-bye. The last sounds I hear are his footsteps out of the house, his car starting up, and the engine revving before slowly fading into nothing.

Just like my voice.

THREE

DIARRHEA, DODGEBALL & SALSA

I'm lying in bed. When I woke up this morning, I had a dad. Not anymore. If I could have just hit the baseball—just a base hit. Even foul-tipped it. No, instead I stood there with the bat on my shoulder and watched three strikes smoke past me. In English, same thing. I couldn't even get the words out, and the only voice that mattered in that classroom was Danny's.

I pull the pillow out from under my head and throw it on the floor. In the darkness Imagination arrives—only this time, not on my team.

Danny: *FAT-TI-CUS! FAT-TI-CUS! FAT-TI-CUS!*

Me: [Silence.]

Danny: *FAT-TI-CUS! FAT-TI-CUS! FAT-TI-CUS!*

Me: [Silence.]

Danny: *FAT-TI-CUS! FAT-TI-CUS! FAT-TI-CUS!*

Me: [Silence.]

I take the blanket off my bed and throw it on the ground as well. I'm cold, but I don't care. Then, suddenly, I can kind of hear this other voice too. Danny still chants, but this other voice is sweet like orange juice. It's sweet like a Boston Cream doughnut. It's sweet like hearing the rain attack your roof, but knowing you're fine because you're in your bed and you're warm and the rain is not going to get you wet.

It's Audrey Higgins. And as soon as my Imagination starts letting her chime in, I can feel myself getting warm again.

Audrey: *Hey, Atticus. You're a pretty awesome guy, you know that?*

Me: *Thanks, that's, uh, you know, that's cool.*

Audrey: *I mean it. It's totally true. I bet one day you'll probably end up being a senator or something crazy like that, doing something really big and important.*

Me: *Uh, yeah, that's cool . . . I mean, yeah, thanks.*

In bed, I can feel my face getting hot and I wonder if I'm blushing. Then I stop wondering, because I know that *I am* blushing and so I close my eyes tightly and pull the blanket and pillow up off of the floor. It's okay. Audrey is here.

But then I hear—

Danny: *FAT-TI-CUS! FAT-TI-CUS! FAT-TI-CUS!*

Audrey is still trying . . . but . . . it's hard to—

Danny: *FAT-TI-CUS! FAT-TI-CUS! FAT-TI-CUS!*

I get up out of bed and turn on my light. I rub my eyes and take a drink of water from the cup sitting on my desk. I look at the walls of my room, as if they'll tell me what I can do to get Danny off my back.

Ever since the fourth grade, Danny has been doing his best to make me feel like crap. No, worse—like diarrhea (which I've had on more than one occasion because of a really nervous stomach, and I know for a fact that it's the most terrible kind of poop known to humankind). His torments started in gym class, when we were playing dodgeball. Even back in fourth grade, I had no athletic ability at all. So in dodgeball, the only thing I had going for me was strategy: hold any ball that came to me until no one else seemed to have one, then run up to the dividing line and launch it as quickly as I could. Then run to the back of the boundary line and roll my body into a tight ball, hoping not to get pegged.

My strategy was working fine until one time I whipped the ball as hard as I could toward the other team. I wasn't aiming—heck, I didn't even know *how* to aim—but the ball managed to find Danny's face just as he was turning. It landed *splat, crack, pop* right on his nose. And the ball ended up breaking his nose. What are the chances? Really? Only my Imagination could have created something like that.

But this was real. Had to be, because I stood there watching all that blood run down Danny's face and all I could think was *Holy crap! Crap, crap, crap, crap. Holy, holy crap!* I couldn't believe that a wuss like me had managed to throw a ball hard enough to break a nose.

Before Danny was taken off the court by Mr. Lamone, Danny looked right at me and said, "You're gonna get it, Fatticus."

Before I broke his nose, Danny was a jerk. He was just never a jerk *to me in particular*. After the dodgeball incident, I became his primary target. "Fatticus" was born, and whatever tiny scraps of respect I had left were gobbled up by the Danny Wills bully machine. It's a wonder that Danny still found time to torment a few other kids.

Which is where Audrey comes in.

Audrey Higgins.

AUDREY HIGGINS!

Just writing her name makes me smile.

She's like a movie on constant replay in my head, and I just watch it over and over again, thinking *wow.*

And let me tell you: there is a lot of *wow* in Audrey Higgins. She has this brownish-reddish hair that lies on her shoulders like a carpet rolling down stairs—you know, the kind they lay out for celebrities. Her smile could light up a whole city. A big city. Like Hartford or maybe even Boston. All you have to do is look at her, and if she gives you one of *those* smiles, you feel as though you're the only person in the entire universe who exists for her.

Yeah, she is *crazy* good-looking, but she's also *crazy good* too. This one time, last year, Danny was picking on a special-ed kid. The kid's name was Beena, and she had this wild hairdo that made her black curls jut out from her head every which way. Beena always had this strange smile on her face, like she was seeing something you never saw. When Beena spoke, it sounded like a dozen people were all trying to talk at the same time and none of them was making sense. Most students simply steered clear of Beena.

But not Audrey.

Any time Audrey saw Beena in the hallways, it was always, "Hi, Beena! How is your day today?" Beena never really seemed to understand, but it didn't stop Audrey from saying it.

Well, this one time on Taco Day, Beena was coming out of the lunch line and Danny was walking right behind her. As Danny passed by Beena, he dumped his little plastic cup of salsa right on her head. I was at the lunch table closest to where it happened, and I could hear him laugh the whole way back to his own table.

Beena started screaming. Just screaming, like she didn't know why her hair was wet and sticky and red all of a sudden. Then Beena dropped to the floor and started spinning around.

My skin itched all over. What I wanted to do was stand up right there in front of the entire lunch room, march on over to Danny, and shout out, *How dare you!* and then whack him hard across the face.

Twice.

No. Three times.

Then I wanted to dump all the salsa in the whole cafeteria on top of him, give him a wedgie the size of California, and whack him three more times.

Instead, my feet felt stapled to the floor. So I sat there. I did nothing.

And that's when it happened: Audrey stood up from her table, practically *ran* over to Danny, and tapped him on the shoulder. When he turned around—still laughing—she slapped him.

Hard.

If I could swing a baseball bat the way Audrey slapped Danny, I'd be a homerun hero. And instead of leaving, my dad would have built a shrine to me in our living room.

Then Audrey went over and put her arm around Beena's shoulder. Finally, Mrs. Harkson made her way over, demanding, "What happened here? What's going on?"

But Audrey just sat there on the floor of the cafeteria hugging Beena. Danny, however, was ready with a story full of the biggest load of crap ever heard by anyone anywhere: Audrey had a secret crush on Danny, explaining the slap; Beena had slipped and fallen, explaining the mess and screaming; Audrey had been helpful to Beena after slapping her crush.

Audrey tried to tell the real version later. But when your mom is on the school board, and your peers are in your back pocket, a story with that much stink to it can become fact. And guess who didn't say anything to support what really happened?

I'm still ashamed about keeping silent. But I'm also in love. Have been since that moment, watching Audrey sit on the floor next to Beena. Maybe because I saw Beena screaming the way I felt like screaming sometimes—and I saw someone who could touch a person that scared without caring what anyone else thought.

FOUR

THE NEW GUY IN TOWN WITH SOGGY FLESH

So, my life is pretty much a mess, and into all of this confusion comes a really, really, really, *really* old guy. His name is Mr. Looney. I'm not even kidding. That's his real name, and he's the oldest guy I have ever seen. When I first meet him Monday morning, his sagging, crinkled skin looks like it's going to fall right off his face and go sliding down his body until it hits the floor in a big puddle of soggy, soppy, old-person flesh.

But that doesn't happen. Instead, the skin stays right on his face while Principal Callahan brings Mr. Looney into our English class and says, "Students, as you know, Mrs. Kathan will be out for a little while. I know that she talked with you all about her maternity leave, and now she needs to be resting at home until the baby is born. For the rest of the school year, your teacher will be Mr. Looney."

The class snickers at the word *Looney*.

"Students!" Mr. Callahan barks. "There'll be none of that. Mr. Looney will get the same kind of respect you have given Mrs. Kathan, is that clear?"

Nobody says anything, and Mr. Callahan must think that means it's clear to us all. Then he nods to Mr. Looney, turns around, and walks out of the classroom.

What Mr. Looney does next is the strangest thing I have ever seen a teacher do in my entire school life. Mr. Looney just stands there, silent, in front of the classroom, for a long, long, long, incredibly long time. I could have watched *The NeverEnding Story* with Adrian in the amount of time Mr. Looney stands there.

And he stares. I mean, he *stares* at all of us like we're aliens. Or like we're covered in chocolate pudding. I don't know—just stares at us like you wouldn't think anyone with soggy flesh would even be *able* to stare. After a while, he starts walking from desk to desk, staring at each student even more closely. Sometimes, he makes this small *hhhmmm* sound—like he's agreeing with himself about something. Then he moves on to the next student.

Danny raises his hand, but Mr. Looney only looks up at Danny like he's—yup—an alien (which is fine by me). Then Mr. Looney keeps looking down, into the eyes of each student. Slowly, one at a time.

Finally, Danny puts his hand down and says out loud, "My name is Danny Wills. Nice to have you as our sub, Mr. Looney. If you have any questions about anything, I can help you out." Danny smiles. I know exactly what he's doing. Everyone in the class does too, I'm sure. Play nice. Pretend. Fool the teachers. Then you can do whatever you want to the other students. It's a strategy that Danny has perfected.

But Mr. Looney completely ignores him—doesn't even look up. It's like Danny never even said anything (which is also fine by me).

"Excuse me, uh, Mr. Looney. I said I can help you out if there's anything you need to know, okay?" Danny's smile looks smaller now.

Again, Mr. Looney ignores him. I start to wonder if my Imagination isn't somehow jumping in here. But when I catch Audrey's eyes, she looks just as amazed as I am.

Danny tries a third time. "Mr. Looney, can you hear me?" He half-yells the words.

Mr. Looney simply moves on to the next student, who happens to be me. I have two thoughts as Mr. Looney stares into my eyes:

Thought #1: *This guy is a psycho. He is supposedly here to teach us, but he is actually mentally unstable and is legally insane. Maybe he WAS sane, once upon a time, but he's certainly lost it now. Maybe he's staring at us so that he can gauge which one of us he'll dissect first, then cook our brains into a big stew and serve it at dinner parties that he hosts on whatever planet he comes from. If this is the case, I hope he cooks Danny's brain first (not that it would taste any good, though, or have much nutritional value).*

Thought #2: *Maybe it was bad with Mrs. Kathan, but now I am REALLY going to get pummeled. At least Mrs. Kathan kept some kind of order in the classroom (however unfair it was). This guy is going to get walked on every day, and if he can't keep the class in line, my fate is seriously in danger. I may not have long to live. To do: write up notes before I die and give them to Mom and Adrian. No note for Dad.*

My mind keeps running in both directions. And I can feel my Imagination undressing down to his bathing suit, ready to dive into the pool of my head.

Then Mr. Looney winks at me.

With his right eye.

Nothing else.

The wink stops everything and makes me see him—I mean *really* see this Mr. Looney guy. His hair is silver, and his eyebrows are like bushes growing above his eyes. He's got a mustache, like my dad, but Mr. Looney's is all white. Stray hairs jump out from it as if they're trying to run away from his face. As he stares at me, it suddenly feels like he can hear my thoughts. Like he's reading me. And if he's reading them right, this is what he's seeing: *What is actually in front of me right now is even crazier than what my Imagination could come up with.*

Then his big green eyes quickly blink, leave me, and go on to the next student.

My mind is strangely calm, and there's only this upstairs right now: *Everything is going to be fine.*

The night after I meet Mr. Looney, I can't sleep. Questions about the soggy-faced substitute teacher are everywhere in my mind: Did he live his entire life up until this *really* old age going around to people and staring into their eyes? He must have earned some sort of teaching certificate, right? Why did he ignore Danny? Why didn't he say ANYTHING?

And then there's The Wink.

What did he mean by it?

It didn't feel like a creepy sort of wink (and trust me, I've seen my fair share of horror movies in which some psycho dentist winks at the innocent patient in his chair before proceeding to drill half his face off, leaving the unsuspecting boy dead in the chair with blood all around before the dentist moves to some brand-new town far away where no one has ever heard of him and he gets another job in a brand-new dentist's office, and all the townspeople think he's great— just *great*—until he drills some other poor, defenseless kid's face off and leaves again, only to repeat the same killing-by-drilling process over and over until the movie people get tired of their own story and the movie ends with him looking into the camera and winking, and saying something like, "Maybe I'll be coming to your town next . . .").

No, nothing like that. Instead, The Wink said to me: *It's okay. I know what you're going through. And trust me, everything is going to work out fine.* But how could someone know what I am going through—all of the junk with my dad and with Danny—without even talking to me once?

The entire English class that first day, all he did was stare at each of us. He stared until the bell rang, and still he didn't say a single word. Not "For homework tonight, write one page introducing yourself to me," and not "Tomorrow, we'll be picking new seat assignments," and not even "I will see you all tomorrow."

Nothing like any other teacher I've ever had. Most teachers, you get a pretty quick sense of who they're going to be in your class.

For starters, there's the *No-Nonsense/Mess-with-Me-and-I'll-Rip-Your-Face-Off-and-Eat-It-for-Breakfast-with-My-Scrambled-Eggs* kind of teacher. This teacher doesn't care what the students think about him; instead, he's happy to know that everyone is pretty much scared beyond belief and will basically do exactly as he says. Usually, what this teacher says to do is worksheets, worksheets, and more worksheets. You wouldn't even *think* about telling this teacher anything about yourself that mattered. As a student, you are supposed to be afraid of this teacher, and that's that.

Then there's the teacher who starts off all nice and sweet and says she wants to be your friend. She says she thinks that the upcoming school year is going to be *magical*, and that as a class you are all going to go on a Journey of Discovery. This teacher is the *Everything-Is-Wonderful-and-I'm-Wonderful-and-You're-Wonderful-and-Isn't-Everything-Just-Wonderful?* sort. That is, until about one or two months into the school year, when everyone is screaming and yelling and seeing who can shoot the rubber bands the farthest across the room, and no one is doing any homework. Then, this Magical Journey teacher pretty quickly turns into something like the first kind of teacher.

The third kind of teacher is the *I'm-Nice-and-You-Can-Relate-to-Me-but-Don't-Mess-with-Me* sort. This teacher usually earns the most respect from students, and basically does a pretty good job. Most of the time, she plans some cool stuff and actually seems to like being in a classroom with us. This kind of teacher usually tries to protect us kids who get bullied a lot too. Problem is, this kind of teacher doesn't happen much.

The last kind of teacher is probably the worst—maybe even worse than the scare-you-to-death first kind. The last kind of teacher is the *I-Don't-Really-Give-a-Darn-about-You* teacher. He couldn't care less about us students, about the subject, about anything really. This kind is the worst because this teacher doesn't hate you or love you—he just doesn't even *see* you.

Right up through eighth grade, I never had a teacher who didn't fall into one of these four categories.

That is, until now.

FIVE

MR. LOONEY WINS A MINOR BATTLE THROUGH JUNGLE MUSIC

On our second day of English class with Mr. Looney, there are no desks.

Seriously.

We all walk into the room, and it's totally empty. I have no clue where Mr. Looney put all of the desks, or why he took them out of the room in the first place. But there we are: twenty-one eighth-grade students ready to complain about doing work, and now this crazy, ancient teacher is beating us to the punch. I guess we won't be doing any writing if there are no desks.

There's also no teacher. Five minutes after the bell rings, Mr. Looney is still missing. We all look at one another like someone has the secret about what's going on but isn't spilling the beans. Even Danny is stunned into silence.

The silence grows long and sticky inside the room. Some of the girls begin to giggle, and a few of the boys start to say things like, "No teacher means no English! We can leave, head for lunch early."

Audrey says, really loudly, that we should tell someone in the main office so they can find a teacher to supervise the class. Most of the boys in the class *booooo* that possibility down immediately.

Danny leads the charge: "That's a dumb idea, a real dumb idea. We don't have a teacher, so we enjoy it, not go get someone else. Hey, maybe the old guy died and the school doesn't know about it. Our chance to have some chill time now!"

A lot of boys start to cheer and high-five each other. I start wondering why boys have to act so tough. It's like there's some secret list of rules every middle-school boy has to follow—all these rules about looking tough, acting tough, not doing what seems to make sense.

Right then, my Imagination grabs hold of me, and all of a sudden I hear this voice-over—like that guy you hear talking during a movie preview, or a sports announcer. But it's so real I can't even hear what Audrey's saying as she starts waving her arms and talking. All I can hear is this guy's loud, happy voice shouting at me:

And now, ladies and gentlemen, it's time for …

The Unspoken Laws for How Eighth Grade Boys at Pitts Middle School Must Act:

- Don't ever look interested in school.
- Don't act like you're smart.
- Don't ever, ever, EVER cry (or, if you do, don't ever, ever, EVER tell anyone that you did).
- If someone does find out that you cried, lie about it. Say that something got caught in your eye. Your dog bit your eye. Your pet parakeet bit your eye. Your little brother bit your eye. Any lie will do: just don't admit that you actually cried. About anything.
- Don't talk to girls.

- If you do talk to girls, act tough. Pretend that your face is actually a block of stone. Pretend that your lips can't actually smile. Act like the guys on the cover of the magazines with ripped muscles: six-pack abs, biceps the size of tree trunks, pecs the size of small villages.

- Don't ever get too excited.

- If you do happen to get too excited, make fun of someone smaller or weirder than you are, and then everyone will forget about how excited you got.

- Be tough. Under no circumstances whatsoever should you ever come across to another human being as sensitive.

- Just to repeat: don't ever cry.

Then, just as quickly as you can say "fart-face," there's a loud crash and the strangest, most exotic music I have ever heard begins to play. It's LOUD. Is this part of the Announcer inside my Imagination? But I look around and everyone else in the room is looking around the same way I feel like I'm looking around. And even Danny and Audrey aren't saying anything—so this must be real.

The only way I can describe the music to you is this: imagine you are lost somewhere in the jungle. All around you are huge trees, hanging vines, and thousands of birds. These birds are flying all over the place—some of them almost hitting you in the head—and they are singing nonstop as they fly around. Below you, there is the darkest soil and the greenest grass you ever saw in your entire life. The dirt is browner than you-know-what, and the grass is brighter and greener than any neon-green store sign that ever existed. Plus, there are monkeys swinging all around you on the hanging vines, and gorillas hunching in groups, and there's even a lion standing in the middle of a path, just standing there and roaring—I mean belting it out as loudly as he possibly can. But none of this makes you feel like you're in any danger. Instead, it all feels alive and peaceful and exciting and new.

The jungle music keeps on playing, until finally a closet door opens in the far back of the classroom. Out from behind the closet door comes Mr. Looney, wearing these ratty jeans with holes in the knees, and some kind of tie-dyed T-shirt. He carries a huge wooden stick and he's hunched over, walking like a cave man or something.

My mouth just drops open. Again, my Imagination is destroyed by reality. Then Mr. Looney begins to belt out animal-like noises mixed in with his own crazy made-up words.

"OOO-SI-MONGOOO . . . OOO-SI-MONGOOO . . . KACHI-CHI! KACHICHI!" These last two words (if you can call them that) ring out louder and more high-pitched than the other sounds. For a teacher who only yesterday seemed unable to speak, these noises feel like thunder bottled up and then set free inside our classroom.

And then—just like yesterday—Mr. Looney begins to hobble toward each student, one at a time. He bends forward to get right in the first girl's face. Margaret. Kind of like me, she never says a single word in class and seems invisible most days. Mr. Looney pauses for a moment and then says, "MARGARET! UH-SA-GU-YAH! KACHICHI-KACHICHI!"

I kid you not: Margaret screams bloody murder. She screams so loud my ears hurt. She must be about to hurl her lunch, or maybe faint, or even take a swipe at Mr. Looney with her fist.

Everyone is waiting to see what's going to happen next. I'm thinking: *What in the heck?! Seriously, what in the heck?! Margaret is going to have a heart attack. Somebody better call an ambulance right now. Mr. Looney is definitely crazy—he has escaped from an insane asylum and he is tormenting us until they take him back to captivity. No wonder his name is Mr. LOONEY!*

But my thoughts are interrupted when Mr. Looney smiles really widely at Margaret, takes her hand in his, and gently pulls her into the center of the classroom. Again, he yells out, "KACHICHI-KACHICHI, MARGARET!" Then he lifts both his arms to the ceiling and points them toward her like he's inviting her to copy him.

What happens next really blows my mind. Margaret does it. I mean, she just lifts both her hands to the ceiling, same as Mr. Looney did.

Then Margaret starts laughing. I mean *laughing*. She laughs so hard that tears roll down her face. Margaret has long black hair, and now that long black hair is becoming all mixed in and mixed up with her tears. When she laughs, her head shakes forward and backward, which only makes things worse. Soon, she's a mess of wildly swinging hair and tears and laughter.

Mr. Looney is laughing with her—this laughter that feels like a train going faster and faster. Then he starts dancing around the room, continuing to raise both his arms up to the ceiling and bring them back down, over and over again.

Just as I'm finally sure that Mr. Looney put out some sort of poisonous gas that makes students do strange and unpredictable things—*how else would the shyest girl in our whole grade start to act this way?*—something even weirder happens.

Margaret actually starts *dancing* around the classroom, following Mr. Looney. The quietest girl in our grade is dancing around a classroom without any desks, raising her hands to the ceiling, following a teacher who looks like he's old enough to be Abraham.

This is the part where I am supposed to write: *And then I woke up, realizing the whole thing was all a dream.*

But instead of waking up, the stranger-than-reality reality continues.

Mr. Looney goes to the next student, Sam, and does the same thing.

"SAM! UH-SA-GU-YAH! KACHICHI-KACHICHI!"

Sam screams as well—not quite as loud as Margaret, but he still lets this shriek rip—and then begins laughing and dancing too. Now, Sam dancing around the room isn't as surprising as Margaret. But still!

I'm watching Mr. Looney, followed by Margaret, followed by Sam, and they're all dancing around the classroom while the jungle music roars. It's like some English class conga line. It totally catches my Imagination off guard. Maybe because I'm trying to figure out if this is even *real*.

Soon, Mr. Looney reaches out a hand and pulls in Audrey. *Audrey Higgins!*

She follows immediately, getting behind Sam, and her head rocks back and her mouth opens wide with laughter. Audrey starts dancing just as crazily as the other three already are, and all I can think is *Man, that looks like fun.* I can't even remember the last time I thought of the word *fun* in the same sentence as anything having to do with school.

They're making loops and circles and wavy lines all over the classroom, and Mr. Looney pulls in a fifth student, Rob, and a sixth, Hannah, and a seventh, Erik. Students just join in like this is all part of the day's lesson plan. Like it's as normal as vocabulary.

Then Mr. Looney turns the conga line *directly toward me*.

His eyes are focused right on my eyes, and again I can see their green sparkle, the bushy eyebrows rising and falling with the rhythm of the music. Mr. Looney leads the line closer to me, and I start to shake. My arms, especially, can't keep still. I'm looking for my Imagination to help me out—to give me some other scene instead of the one I'm in—but still it's silent. It's not giving me anything other than what's right in front of me. And what's right in front of me is: Mr. Looney's dancing eyebrows; Mr. Looney's steady green eyes; Mr. Looney's wrinkly face.

As he leads the conga line closer to me, I can feel time slow down. You know how in movies they always have these slow-motion scenes, like when somebody shoots a basket right before the buzzer? Well, everything feels like that, except I haven't shot any basketball—I haven't done *anything* except stand, terrified, in front of Mr. Looney and the conga line.

Then he's *here*. He reaches out and takes my hand. As soon as Mr. Looney's wrinkly hand grabs mine, my feet tumble forward, and I'm heading toward the line myself.

While I'm still not sure exactly what I'm doing, I feel another hand grab mine and pull me completely into the conga line.

Audrey.

As we make our way around the room, Mr. Looney continues pulling students into the line, and as the music roars and everyone is moving, dancing, yelling, I forget about Danny Wills.

I forget, too, that I am a wuss.

By the time the bell rings to end our second day of class with Mr. Looney as our long-term substitute English teacher, almost the entire class is dancing and making strange noises.

OO-BAYUH!

JUJUJUJUJU!

DONOTIKI!

FELURA-TURA-DURA!

ZZZZZZAPATAPPA!

KACHICHI-KACHICHI!

But Danny doesn't do a single thing. He doesn't dance, doesn't yell, doesn't talk. He can't get anyone to stand there with him on the side of the room, so he just stands there by himself.

The last time I see Danny that day, he's leaving the classroom where all of us are quickly losing whatever marbles we had rolling around in our heads. Danny yells something that is drowned out by the jungle music, and then he slams the classroom door.

It seems like Mr. Looney doesn't even notice Danny has left. Instead, he just keeps dancing like a crazy cave man.

Two thoughts run through my mind:

How can this older-than-dirt guy have enough energy to run around the room screaming for almost forty-three minutes and not fall down dead?

Whatever happened in class today somehow pissed off Danny, and I like it. I like it a lot.

No homework.
No discussion.
No reading.
No textbooks.
No spelling quizzes.
No seating assignments.

And that is day number two of English class with Mr. Looney.

six

MONKEYS, LIONS, AND INJUSTICE

It's the first weekend after Mr. Looney has been in for Mrs. Kathan. My dad is officially gone on his "Figure-Myself-Out" thing. My mom, my brother, and I are sitting around in the living room trying to decide what to do on our first Saturday without my dad.

"Well, how about we head over to the zoo? Remember how much you loved the zoo the last time we went, Atticus?" My mom smiles, like she's trying to pretend that nothing has really changed.

"Mom—the zoo is for little kids. Maybe a twerp like Adrian would like it, but not me. Why can't I just do my own thing?"

I'm still angry at my dad for leaving us, but I can't just call him up and tell him how pissed I am.

"I am not a twerp! *You're* the twerp! Twerp! Twerp-face!" Adrian looks at me like I've just rubbed his face in dog poop.

"Atticus, don't talk to your brother like that, please." My mom looks at me like, *Can you at least try to be happy?*

And all I want to roar back is, *No!*

Instead, I look at Adrian and then at my mom. "Fine," I say. "Let's go to the zoo."

The thing about the zoo is this: when you're going there to escape the fact that your dad left you, and everyone in your family is trying to pretend that everything is wonderful, it really sucks.

When I was little, I used to love the zoo—especially the lions' den. As soon as we arrived, I'd be pulling on my dad's shirt, begging him and my mom to go to the lions' den first. I could stand there in front of those thick metal bars all day, watching the lions stalk back and forth across their terrain. They always looked so powerful. But they also seemed peaceful—like they *knew* they were strong and didn't have to show it off. I mean, they weren't in their den ripping apart prey or anything.

Today, as soon as we get to the zoo, my mom asks, "Interested in checking out the lions, Atticus?"

"Maybe when I was five or six, but not anymore. The lions are stupid."

Adrian yells out, "Let's get popcorn balls and then go see the monkeys!" He loves popcorn balls. Anywhere we go, the first thing he wants to do is get a popcorn ball. I don't get it, it's just a massive ball of butter, sugar, and corn. That's it. A stupid ball of stuff mushed together—what is there to be so magically excited about?

"Popcorn ball it is," my mom says, still smiling.

Adrian doesn't know our dad has left us for good. My mom told me that she had "a talk" with him, but that she said dad was just taking a little break—like going on a long trip. I have no clue when mom will tell him that dad is gone for good, but I sure hope she stocks the house with plenty of popcorn balls.

Once we reach the monkeys, popcorn balls in hand, we stand there and watch them swing all over the place.

"Look at that one! Look at that one!" Adrian yells. He's pointing at the biggest monkey I have ever seen. If some zoo-keeper came along and said, *That's actually not a monkey, young lad, that's a hippopotamus,* I'd completely believe him. The monkey has got gobs of body hanging off his, well, body, and when he swings from one tree branch to another, the branches bend and creak with his weight.

The hippo monkey is making the rounds among the smaller monkeys, sometimes taking whatever food they're nibbling on, sometimes looking like he's saying something to them, and then moving on to another tree, other monkeys.

Adrian keeps pointing and yelling, and the sound of him chomping on his popcorn ball makes me want to plug my ears. Instead, as I stand there watching that monkey, my Imagination kicks in. And suddenly, I can hear what the hippo monkey says to the other monkeys.

Hippo Monkey: *Hey, Little Worm.*

Small Monkey: *Aw, come on. I gave you my food the last time Zoo-Man brought it to us. You said I only had to give you one of my meals a day. Can't you find someone else to get some food from?*

Hippo Monkey: *Are you questioning my decision?* [Takes a swipe at Small Monkey's arm—the one that holds the food.]

Small Monkey: [Visibly afraid.] *No, of course not. I would never question your decision. I'm just saying that maybe you could get some food from someone else . . . you know?*

Hippo Monkey: *Listen here, you little worm. I'm getting this meal from you, whether you like it or not. You understand me? Or do you need me to sit on your face again and let one rip?*

Small Monkey: [Does not respond.]

Hippo Monkey: *That's what I thought.* [Reaches out and takes the food from the small monkey.]

Small Monkey: [Swings away to another tree, head down.]

The more I watch the big monkey, the more I keep hoping one of those branches will break and he'll fall and crack his head open.

Meanwhile, Adrian's popcorn ball is being demolished by his mouth, and in between chomps he keeps shouting, "Look at him! He eats so much food!" He points as the hippo monkey swings from tree to tree.

"Yes, he sure is a large one." My mom isn't even looking at the monkeys. She's standing behind Adrian, looking at something that isn't even there. "How's your popcorn ball?" she asks Adrian.

"Awesome! The best popcorn ball ever!"

"That's good, honey."

Then, behind us, some zoo guide clears his throat. He smiles really big at me when I turn to look at him. He's got light brown hair, and he's wearing a bright red jacket with a badge that says, I'M FRANK. ASK ME ANYTHING!

I think about what I *really* want to ask Frank, and I make this list in my mind:

Questions I Really Want to Ask Frank but Certainly Will Not:

- Why do fathers leave their kids?
- Why do little brothers love popcorn balls and farting so much?
- How do you deal with a school bully who is twice your size and has about ten times as much courage as you do?
- What are you supposed to do with really, really, really old teachers who dance around the

classroom to jungle music?

- How do you ask out a girl who is beautiful—I mean, stunning and gorgeous and every other adjective you can think of—even when you're seen as a wuss by most kids in the school?

Instead of asking Frank any of these questions, I just keep quiet.

"Hi, folks, having a good day today at the zoo?" Frank looks way too happy.

"Yeah! Look at this awesome monkey!" Adrian roars back at Frank, as if Frank has no idea it exists.

"Oh, yes, that's Mojani. He's quite a monkey. He loves it when people watch him, and he's always on the move. He's certainly a favorite of the zoo's guests." Frank waves to the hippo monkey as if he will wave back.

I cringe.

Even though I wasn't going to say anything, suddenly I can't help it. The hippo monkey is everybody's favorite? Really?

"But the hippopotamus-monkey takes the food from all the smaller monkeys! How can that make him a favorite? Isn't that wrong?" By the end of my so-called question, I feel as though I am yelling. But Frank's leaning in, like he can barely hear me.

Even when I want to scream, my voice only trickles out of my mouth.

Frank smiles. "Oh no, not at all! See, there's an order to the natural world, and monkeys are just a part of that world. The other monkeys know that Mojani is a leader, and they enjoy being under his control. He helps to bring a certain clarity to their lives. They follow him, and he keeps them under control. All part of the natural order of life."

I really, really want to say to Frank: *Natural order?! How come anything wrong that someone does is part of the natural order? Isn't justice part of the natural order too?*

Instead, I swallow hard and walk away, leaving Frank to wonder what's wrong with the strange, short boy.

When we finally get to the lions' den, I can't believe what I see. The lions look like somebody gave them a bunch of sedatives. I mean, they're just laying around on these rocks and fake mountains doing nothing.

Absolutely nothing.

There's no way these are the same kind of lions I saw when I was a kid. These lions look so . . . defeated.

Zoned out.

Depressed.

Adrian is on his fourth popcorn ball of the day.

"Remember, Atticus, how much you used to love the lions? Every time we came here, you always wanted to stay right in front of this den the entire day. No matter what we said, we could never convince you to leave it." My mom looks *almost* happy for a moment. "I remember one time, your dad said he wanted to visit some other sections of the zoo, and I told him to go. He left, and you and I just stood here for hours. Everything the lions did, you pointed out to me. You loved the lions more than anything I've ever seen."

It's the first time she's mentioned my dad to me since he left. I think she only does it because it's a memory that was good without him.

"I don't remember that day," I lie. I'm pissed at my dad, but I'm just not ready to let him go.

My mom looks away fast, like she's about to start crying.

"Can we leave?" I ask.

Walking away, I take one last look at the lions. I think to myself: *All that strength. All wasted.*

SEVEN

STAINS AND PERFECT MEMORIES

Most of that first weekend without my dad, all I can do is ask myself questions about why he really left us.

Did my mom do something stupid to make him walk out? Did he just get tired of Adrian's ridiculous farting-noise obsessions? Or—my worst thought—was it me? Did I do something to make my dad leave? Did I strike out one too many times in baseball? Was I not as smart as he'd wanted? Not tall enough? Not confident enough?

I try as hard as I can to remember some of the things my dad used to do with me when I was younger. How did we spend time together? I can remember throwing the baseball back and forth in the backyard. But it was always, *Throw harder, Atticus! Throw faster, Atticus!* No matter what, it always seemed like I could be a little bit better.

Another memory flashes to my mind: After one of our baseball games, my dad went up to Danny and said, "Wow, Danny, you sure played a great one today! Nine strikeouts and three base hits. Maybe Atticus will play like that one day."

Danny responded, "Atticus will *never* play like that . . . he's pretty terrible." And then—I remember this as clear as anything—my dad said absolutely nothing. Here's Danny, snotty-nosed jerk that he is, saying to *my dad* that I suck at baseball, and what does my dad do?

Nothing.

Absolutely nothing.

As I think about that day, something in me feels broken. So I try to *not* think about it. But once it comes to my mind, it keeps me up late into Saturday night. So I figure if I'm going to be awake thinking about this awful memory, I might as well re-create it the way I wish it would have happened. So I open the door to my Imagination, and here's the version I like best (because when you can't sleep at night, there's an awful lot of time to come up with an awful lot of versions):

Dad: *Wow, Danny, did you know that the whole time you were pitching and hitting today, your tightey-whitey underwear was showing?*

Danny: *No, Mr. Hobart, I didn't know that . . . but it doesn't matter. I still pitched and hit a great game, unlike your son, Atticus, who pretty much stunk up the field.*

Dad: *I don't know, Danny. See, from the look of the stains you had on your underwear, I would guess that any stinking up of the field was probably accomplished by you. Did you forget to wipe or something before you pulled up your pants and came to the ballgame today?*

Danny: [Growing very angry.] *Shut up!*

Dad: *Danny, I think maybe you need to shut your underwear up—real tight, somewhere no one will ever be able to find that nasty-smelling stuff you're wearing. And while you're at it, maybe you could try wiping the next time you use the bathroom. It's not terribly difficult. All you have to do is take some toilet paper, wad it up good, then scrub back and forth, and poof—no stains on your underwear. Imagine that!*

Danny: *You're so mean. You shut up! Shut up!*

Dad: *Danny, I'm not mean at all—see, I'm just trying to help you out. I don't want you to have to keep pitching and hitting with such a mess all over yourself.*

Danny: [Runs away crying.]

Yeah, I admit, my dad is kind of a jerk in my Imagination's version—but he's a jerk *to Danny Wills*. And I also will tell you this: it helps me finally fall asleep on Saturday (and Sunday) night.

But when I wake up Monday morning, the question I can't get out of my head is: How am I going to make it without a dad?

Even if he only cared about how well I did at baseball, at least he was still my dad. At least he was *here*. Now, there's nothing. No one. And on my way to school Monday morning, I can't figure out what's worse: having a crappy dad who doesn't really like you much or not having a dad at all.

EIGHT

THE ONE THING

Monday morning.

9:17 a.m.

Mr. Looney utters his first comprehensible human words. He says, "It is truly wonderful to be here with you all."

Then he gets into his non-speaking-comprehensible-words-mode again. He looks around at all of us. Everyone's silent. Even Danny has fallen into a bit of a daze. Like the rest of us, he's waiting to see what Mr. Looney will say next.

Just as suddenly, Mr. Looney speaks again. "I am seventy-seven years old. I have taught forty-nine years of students just like you. And I have learned one thing. Only *one* thing." I can't believe this voice belongs to a seventy-seven-year-old man. It's clear, loud, and strong. It's the kind of voice that, when you hear it, you think to yourself: *I'd better listen up. This voice has got something interesting to say.* It's also the kind of voice that makes you think, *I don't want to hear what this voice could do if I* don't *listen to it.*

Then Mr. Looney stares us all down as he slowly lifts his right index finger up above his head. I glance quickly to my left. Hannah Quill is leaning forward in her chair, like she's going to collapse before Mr. Looney gets to tell us what the "one thing" is.

Mr. Looney moves his finger from right to left and back a few times. Then he says again, "Just *one* thing."

Hannah's gum falls clear from her mouth and lands on the desk with a *splat*. The thought bubble above all of our heads reads: WHAT IS THE *ONE* THING YOU LEARNED? WHAT?! WHAT THE HECK IS IT?! TELL US! TELL US! TELL US!

Of course, it isn't cool to be too interested in anything a teacher has to say. You don't win anyone's respect in the eighth grade by being eager to jump into what the teacher is doing.

Then again, we've never had a teacher quite like Mr. Looney.

Finally, it's too much. Sam belts out, "Well, what did you learn, Mr. Looney?"

And no one in the class seems to care that Sam speaks out.

"I'll tell you," Mr. Looney begins. "But you have to promise that no matter what, *under any circumstances*, you will never mention this to me again. I can only tell you this once, and that's that. No questions about it, no clarifications, no *whaddaya means*, no elaborating."

"What's elbarating?" Hannah asks, a new stick of gum in her mouth.

Mr. Looney walks over to Hannah. "Please stand up, Hannah." She does. "Now, is it true that your hair is red?" Mr. Looney asks her.

"It's totally true that my hair is red. And it's beautiful." Hannah has no problem talking about herself like that—it usually makes the rest of the class laugh and everyone seems to find her friendly enough.

"Well," Mr. Looney continues. "If I said that your hair is red like the sun in the early morning before the summer day gets hot, when the slightest tips of the smallest clouds touch that early light and make it the richest red anyone could ever see . . . would that also be true?"

Hannah blushes.

"Well, then," Mr. Looney finishes. "The second way I described your hair would be *elaborating*. I gave a lot more details to explain what kind of *red* your hair is."

Hannah sits down, smiling. "But Mr. Looney . . . what about the *one thing*?"

"Ah, yes, back to the *one thing*. Here it is: the one thing. But again, you must promise not to ask me *any* questions after I've told you. I will simply share the one thing, and then we'll move on to our first book as if I haven't said a word. Is that clear?"

We all nod. Some of us even mutter *yes* under our breath.

"Okay, then, here goes." He pauses again. "But before I tell you, there's one more thing . . ."

Finally, a laugh rises up out of us. It's the first time I feel I might have something of a handle on what this Mr. Looney is all about. So far, he's shocked and confused us—and no one could have said he bored us—but now he's shown he can be funny too.

When our laughter dies down, Mr. Looney says, "The one thing I've learned is this: we are most afraid of ourselves."

True to our agreement, we don't ask a single question. In fact, it's kind of the opposite. A lot of my classmates look like, *Well, that was kind of a stupid thing to wait all that time for*. But for me, the words hit something inside me that needed to hear a line like that.

Danny mutters from the back of the room, "Garbage—bunch of stupid garbage."

Hannah's blush has faded and she pops her gum.

Audrey, just in front of me, nods her head. I can't tell what expression she's got on her face, but I imagine that she's as much into the one thing as I am. Then, before I can help it, this is the scene my Imagination flashes:

Audrey: *Atticus, you seem like a brilliant guy; what do you make of the* one thing *Mr. Looney shared in class today?* [Audrey brushes against my shoulder as we walk home from school together.]

Me: *Oh, I'm glad you asked, Audrey. Well, I think it means that what's inside of us can be scarier than what's outside of us.*

Audrey: *That's deep, Atticus.*

Me: *Thanks, Audrey.*

Audrey: *I mean, that is the deepest thing I have ever heard before. Wow. I am flabbergasted and amazed. You have an incredible mind. I bet you're probably one of the smartest living eighth-graders on the planet.* [Audrey stops and looks me full in the face, as if she's hoping I'll lean toward her and plant one right on her lips. She blushes.]

Me: *Thanks, Audrey. I think you are brilliant too. And beautiful. You are the most beautiful girl in the world. Anywhere. Ever.*

Audrey: *And you're the hottest guy ever. You are a stud-muffin, Atticus, a blueberry stud-muffin, and you are the most attractive guy I have ever met in my entire life, and I love blueberries and I love stud-muffins—especially those blueberry stud-muffins who are also brilliant and deep—and you are all of these things . . . so . . . I guess what I'm saying is . . .* [Audrey leans closer to me.] *I . . .* [she closes her eyes] *love . . .* [she brings her lips together and leans all the way forward, and just before she kisses me . . . .] *you.*

BAM!

[The most magical kiss that has ever occurred in the history of kissing occurs right there on Felton Street, just a few blocks away from the school.]

Me: *Wow, Audrey, that was incredible . . . so, I guess I'm your boyfriend now, huh?* [I smile wide.]

Audrey: *I guess so.* [Audrey laughs then blushes.]

I snap back to reality as Mr. Looney pulls his chair into the center of the classroom, sits down, and then looks at all of us. He speaks again.

"When you met me, you thought I was old and crazy, right?"

Hannah yells out, "Uh, yeah!" and blushes just a little. But Mr. Looney only smiles in return.

He continues. "You had good reason to think I was crazy—and good reason to think that I was old." He pauses a moment here and winks at me, as if to say, *Yup, I know what you were thinking.*

"The thing you didn't realize is that when I stared at each of you, and when I swooped and whooped around the classroom like a caveman, I was trying to help you take off some of the layers of what you learned school is supposed to be all about."

Mr. Looney pushes back his chair and stands up—straight and strong. My eyes are fixed on him.

"See, all of us are afraid of ourselves, and if we just keep going through our days the way we normally do, we never get underneath the layers to even find out what we're afraid of! It's like we spend our whole lives hiding and pretending to be people we're not. And that, students, is the truly *crazy* thing to do: live your whole life without ever finding out what you really think, what's inside you, and what you believe."

I keep wondering to myself, *Is this guy for real?* I've never heard a teacher talk like this before.

Mr. Looney goes and stands behind his chair; then he picks it up and thumps it down for emphasis. "That's why I stared at you all: to get you to open your eyes, to feel what it's like to be *really* looked at, to be *really* seen by someone."

Sam blurts out, "And why the jungle thing, Mr. Looney?"

"Good question," Mr. Looney says. "But let me ask you a question in return, instead of directly answering yours, if that's okay."

"Sure," Sam says.

"Did my *jungle thing* shock you and make you wonder what was going on?"

"More than anything that's ever happened to me in school!" Sam immediately responds.

"Well, there you go. I wanted you to begin to get the sense that school doesn't have to be what it has always been. Just because things are a certain way, that doesn't make them always right." Mr. Looney sits down.

I have so many thoughts and questions that I feel my head actually bubbling—words seem like they will shoot out of me if I would just dare open my mouth.

I don't.

Instead, I roll the *one thing* around in my mind.

We are most afraid of ourselves.

NINE

A NEW BURNING DESIRE

After our second week with Mr. Looney—and my second week without my dad at home—my new teacher has me hooked. Anything the guy says I eat up like it comes straight from the mouth of God. He manages to hook a lot of us like that.

Most people expect an old person to be kind of out of it. I mean, you walk by old people homes and you think, *That's where all the old people go when they're getting ready to die.* But then someone like Mr. Looney shows up, and the idea of being *old* becomes something entirely different.

I want to go up and talk to him after class—ask him about his life, where he came from, and how he manages to bounce around the classroom at seventy-seven years old. But I'm embarrassed and don't know what to say.

That is, until I see Audrey chatting up a storm with Mr. Looney one day after class. I pretend to have trouble getting all my books together just so I can stick around longer to try to catch a few words.

I can't hear everything from where I'm sitting, so the parts I do hear sound incredibly confusing. What I can make out goes something like this:

Mr. Looney: "Yes, I think that's quite true, Audrey. But is there any other purpose you can think of? Any other . . ." [Here, Mr. Looney turns his head to put a book in his bag and I miss the end of what he says.]

Audrey: "Well, maybe because of money? Or fame? I mean, an author gets pretty famous most of the time, right?"

Mr. Looney: "Ha-ha-ha." [No, his laugh isn't quite a "ha-ha" kind of laugh. Here, let me try again. *Ho-ho-ho.* No, he isn't Santa Claus standing there laughing. It's more of a deep laugh that also rises to a bit of a high pitch. One more try. *Ha-ho-he.* Okay, it looks like I'm not going to be able to capture the exact sound of Mr. Looney's laugh, so just believe me when I say that it is the kind of laugh that makes you feel like you want to laugh too. I guess some sounds you just can't make again—some sounds you have to be there to hear.]

Audrey: "What's so funny?"

Mr. Looney: "It's something much deeper than money or fame. The other reason an author writes a book . . ." [Here, again, Mr. Looney's words fade out. Only this time it's because he bends toward Audrey and whispers the reason into her ear. Then Audrey's eyes light right up.]

Audrey: "Thanks, Mr. Looney—thanks a ton. I'm going to get started on my book right away—and I know just the purpose to get me to finish it now."

Audrey wants to write a book? *A book?!* What eighth-grade kid writes a book? Somehow, this new fact only grows my already enormous, larger-than-life, smash-a-freight-train, stronger-than-the-Incredible-Hulk crush on her.

But there's something else too. I now feel this new, burning desire to know a second thing from Mr. Looney:

Why *does* an author write a book?

At lunch, I feel a smack on the back of my head. When I turn around, it's Danny. *Great. Just when things start looking up.*

"Listen, Fatticus. You think you're safe because of this stupid Looney geezer? I know you love him. But I don't care what you or anyone else thinks of him—that classroom is *mine*, okay? You better just cut out all that googly-eyed staring and smiling."

Usually, whenever Danny starts messing with me, I just try to do whatever he wants, hoping it won't get any worse.

So I'm not sure where I find the words, but they're there— even if they're quiet as anything. "I like Mr. Looney, even if you don't."

I feel another hard smack. *Where are the teachers when you need them?!*

"You like what I tell you to like. Watch your back, Fatticus." And before I realize what I've done or how the words even got out of my mouth, Danny is gone.

All that hangs where he was is a threat.

TEN

THE TUNNEL TO HEAVEN AND HELL

Saturday morning.

I wake up before my mom and Adrian so I can walk to the tunnel near our house, back behind a vacant lot where someone long ago cleared a space to build a home. For some reason, no builders ever showed up, so no house was ever built. When I was little—maybe seven or eight—exploring that vacant lot was pretty much the definition of adventure.

I'd had a few friends over the day we stumbled upon the tunnel (which, we later found out, was actually part of the city's sewer system), and we just started walking inside of it. Of course, it was pitch black inside of there, and we got so scared we could have peed our pants. So we ran right back out again.

From that day on, though, almost every time we got together, we would go exploring in that tunnel. Each time, we tried to get a little bit farther than the last and commemorate our progress with a chalk mark. One day, we made it far enough to see that at the end of the first tunnel were two more tunnels. Most of our parents had made us go to church, and it seemed everyone there talked about heaven and hell an awful lot, so we didn't need anyone to tell us where those two tunnels *actually* led. And from then on, the tunnel was known as the Tunnel to Heaven and Hell.

Before his dad got a new job in Oregon, one of my friends, Adam, and I used to come to the tunnel a lot. Even though it's been at least four or five years since I've been back to the tunnel, when it comes into view now, the way Adam and I would talk about it comes alive in my head. I can hear us talking like we are still eight years old, and right here.

Me: *So, what are you going to ask God when we take the tunnel to heaven?*

Adam: *I'm thinking of heading down to hell first, you know? I want to see how big the flames are down there! Plus, we could see who's down there—like, maybe anyone we know? I think my uncle Marcus is probably down there. He hit a dog with his car and then drove away and left the dog there in the road, whimpering and hobbling. I was in the backseat, 'cause he took me to McDonald's PlayPlace, and he said to me, "Whoops, Adam . . . looks like we hit a big rock."*

Me: *He must have thought you were pretty dumb to believe that a dog was actually a rock.*

Adam: *Yeah, he must've thought I was pretty dumb to believe that a dog was a rock.*

Me: *Yeah.*

Adam: *Yeah. So, you wanna check out hell first and point at my uncle Marcus and then head up to heaven and see God?*

Me: *Sounds good to me, but I've got to make sure I'm back by six or else my mom will go nuts.*

Adam: *Yeah, me too—six. I hope God doesn't talk too much, 'cause then it would be hard to get away in time for dinner.*

Me: *Yeah.*

I don't know exactly why I'm coming here again today. Why, after so many years, I decided to get up early and walk to an old sewer.

As I get closer, I can't believe that my friends and I ever played here and thought it was fun. The tunnel is dirty. It smells funky. The water running along the bottom is more like a trickle than the rushing tide I remember. I laugh out loud at how stupid I was when I was younger. I actually believed this ridiculous sewer was something special.

I start to wonder if this is the way life really works out: you think everything's great when you're a little kid. Your dad tells you he loves you, your mom tells you she loves you, you draw pictures, and you see a sewer and pretend it can lead you to heaven and hell if you ever decide to become a tourist and take the trip.

Then, you grow up and realize that's all a load of crap. Your parents decide they're going to get divorced; you get bullied at school because you're a mime compared to everyone else; and you've got the World's Worst Name.

I try to force myself to see that sewer as some kind of crazy adventure again. I try to let go of all the stuff that is eating away at me and just remember what it was like to be little again—to have fun. I stand there and stare at that tunnel until my eyes and my head ache from staring.

No matter how hard I try, all I can see is a dirty, old sewer.

ELEVEN

DANNY WILLS FINDS A PUNCHING BAG

On my way back across the vacant lot, it's just my luck that I happen to meet Danny.

I try to avoid him, walking way around the right side of the lot with my head down and hoping he won't notice me. It's no use.

My ears tingle, and I feel my toes curl into the bottoms of my shoes when I hear Danny's voice lunge across the lot toward me: "Hey, Wuss!"

I run. I figure that I might have a shot at making it back to my house before Danny gets his ugly hands on me. It's a longshot, I know, but I have to make some kind of effort to save my own life.

"Hey, Fatticus!" Danny's not going to let me go; he starts running. He catches up to me before I even make it out of the vacant lot.

"Danny—just leave me alone, I have to get home. My mom needs me. I have to watch my brother." The excuses pour out of me. Maybe if I keep talking, I'll find some reason that he'll accept.

But do I really expect him to respect anything I say? Like Danny will listen to me and just say, *Oh, sorry about that, Atticus. I didn't realize that you needed to help your mom today. Maybe I can pummel you another time. Here, let me just take out my calendar . . . let's see . . . I have an opening next Tuesday after school. Would that time work for you? No? Hmmmm, let's see, I do have a fairly full schedule these days with so many dorks to beat up, but I'm sure I can get you into another time slot since you're in such a rush today.*

"Really, Danny, really—I have to go. I've really got to get home and help my mom."

He just laughs. "Fatticus has to help Mommy. *Oh, Mommy, Dwarf-Boy is here to help! Fatticus to the rescue!*" Danny pushes me backward, and I realize that this is it. There's no one around to help.

Before I can say another word, he throws his fist right into my stomach. It's like somebody reaches in and grabs my breath and pulls it right out of me. I curl forward, clutching my stomach, and then I cough.

When I can stand up again, I look at Danny and see that his eyes are like fire.

"You think you can tell me you like a teacher—you think *you* can tell me anything, Fatticus? You do what I tell you to do. That's all."

He's never hit me like this. He's called me names, shoved me, slapped the back of my head—but nothing this bad. My body tightens up. I don't know if he's done, or if there's more coming.

I start walking backward, my eyes still on him.

"You leave when I say you can leave, Fatticus." Danny takes two steps and throws his knee into my stomach. It hits me almost exactly where his fist did. I fall to the ground.

All I can do is cough and cough and cough, and I wonder if I'm spitting up blood.

Then nothing for a moment. When I think maybe it's all over, I lift my head and start to roll over onto my back. Above me, I see two hands holding gobs of grass and dirt. The mess explodes all over my face, and with it I feel something wet.

Danny wipes the last of the spit off his mouth. His shoulders rise and fall with laughter.

It's over.

For a long time after Danny leaves, I lay on the ground. I look up at the sky. There are no answers written in the clouds.

I've seen so many movies about kids my age getting bullied—read so many books too. Someone always comes along to save the defenseless kid. Just at the last moment, when the beating seems inevitable, some hero jumps into the scene and saves the day.

When I finally pick myself up off the ground, I feel a drizzling rain. It's like the sky is crying the tears I'm too angry to shed.

TWELVE

MY STOMACH THINKS IT'S THE DECISION-MAKER IN THIS RELATIONSHIP

For the rest of that weekend, I stay in my room. Adrian knocks on my door once or twice, asking me to watch *The NeverEnding Story* or ride bikes with him. I yell back at him, "Shut up!" and "Leave me alone!" I feel kind of bad about being mean to him. But maybe this is how the world works. People treat each other like crap, and whoever is the best at treating everyone else like crap gets to be respected.

I mean, it seems to work for my dad, right? He leaves me, my mom, and Adrian—treats us like crap—and he's probably off watching baseball games, living it up.

And it seems to work for Danny, right? He treats Beena, me, and anyone he wants to like crap, and he gets respect from everybody.

But then two people immediately come to my mind for which this Treat-Everyone-Like-Crap mentality doesn't seem to fit: Audrey and Mr. Looney.

Audrey treats everyone like they're some kind of treasure. And Mr. Looney seems to actually *like* all of his students. He seems to think we're the exact opposite of crap—even a wuss like me who can barely speak.

As I am considering the *Crap vs. No Crap* debate in my mind, my mom's voice comes through my locked door.

"Atticus, there's pizza for dinner tonight."

I take her words as a peace offering. When I got back from getting pummeled by Danny yesterday, my mom flipped. She was angrier than I'd seen her in a long time. She wanted to call the police, file a report, get Danny arrested. I convinced her that doing that would only make my life even more miserable. If she forced me to tell the cops, Danny would never let me forget it.

Then she got angry at *me*, asking, "Did you do anything to start this whole thing? What happened? There must be some reason why he hates you so much, isn't there?"

When she gets angry (or also when she is just plain curious) my mom can ask a thousand questions without taking a single breath. I don't know, maybe God is up there giving each mom a special Rapid-Fire Questioning Ability as soon as their babies are born, because it seems like every mother in the history of the planet can do this.

After we argued for a long time about what to do, my mom finally agreed to let it go as long as I told a teacher at school about the situation and asked for help. I promised that I would tell one of my teachers. I don't know *how* I'm going to bring it up with Mr. Looney, but I want to talk to him anyway, and maybe this is a way to get the conversation going.

So I yell through the door to my mom. "What kind of pizza did you get?"

"Your favorite—sausage and meatball."

I feel my mouth water. Then my stomach lunges for the door like it has its own brain, its own legs even. I want to stay mad—stay furious at Danny, and my dad, and my mom, and my little brother for being so annoying, and the world in general—but my stomach keeps pushing me toward that sausage and meatball pizza. My Imagination kicks in, and suddenly I am having a conversation with my own stomach.

Me: *But I'm still really pissed at EVERYONE.*

Stomach: *That's fine, man, but don't make me suffer because you're angry at the world.*

Me: *Whoever died and made you King of Our Decisions?*

Stomach: *Look, man, I'm not saying I'm the King of Our Decisions . . . but I am saying that I'm the King of All Our Decisions Concerning Food. After all, I've had thirteen years on this earth as a stomach, and I've done a pretty good job, I think.*

Me: *So do I have any say in this matter whatsoever?*

Stomach: *Not really, man. One way or another, I am going to get my intestines on all those steamy sausages, all those perfectly rounded meatballs, all that gooey, stretchy, sizzling cheese, all that tasty bread! That tasty bread! That tasty bread!*

Me: *Stomach, you've lost it. You are officially insane.*

Stomach: *Tasty bread! Tasty bread! Tasty bread!*

Me: *Stomach, stop it!*

Stomach: *Tasty bread! Tasty bread! TASTY BREAD!*

Then I lose the battle.

THIRTEEN

MINIVAN CHAOS & SAGGY FACES

On Monday, I get to school twenty minutes early. My mom pulls into the parking lot all in a huff because I've changed my mind and now I don't want to talk with Mr. Looney about the whole Danny-beating-me-up thing.

"Look, Atticus, we talked about this and we decided that you would talk to a teacher about it today."

"I know what I said, Mom. But everything's fine now. It's no big deal anymore." Some of the scratches on my face have lost their color. The bruises are still there, but no one can see those through my clothes.

"Atticus—just do it, will you!?" My mom seems exhausted. If I decide to fight this one out, I'll win. I can sense it.

"Yeah, Atticus, just do it! Just do it!" From the backseat of the van, Adrian yells again and again.

"Shut up, Adrian—for once!" I roar back at him.

"Shut up, Adrian—for once!" he copies me in a high-pitched squeal.

"Adrian, don't copy your brother!" my mom yells.

"Adrian, don't copy your brother!" Adrian copies.

"Shut up!" I yell.

"Shut up!" Adrian says.

"Adrian—stop it this instant, or else there will be serious consequences for you, and I mean it!" my mom stammers.

"Adrian—stop it this instant—" Adrian begins but is interrupted when my mom screams.

"I can't take it anymore! I CAN'T TAKE IT ANYMORE!" It's louder than I've ever heard her scream before.

Then there's a knock on my window. Even though it's silent in the car now, my mom's scream feels like it's still *here*. I look over. It's the saggy face of Mr. Looney. He smiles at me then gestures for me to roll down the window. I look at my mom. Her face is in her hands.

I press the power button to roll down the window. My mom's face shoots up. Before she can say anything, Mr. Looney speaks.

"Morning, Atticus. Want to join me on my way into the school?" His voice is calm and quiet. My mom takes a breath and tries to smile like everything is fine.

"Morning, Ma'am," Mr. Looney says. Then he tips the front of his beige hat toward my mom.

"Good morning. Are you the substitute English teacher while Mrs. Kathan is on maternity leave?" It's amazing. If I hadn't seen it myself, I wouldn't believe that only a moment before, my mom was screaming so loudly.

"That I am, Ma'am. Robert Looney is the name, and I'm very glad to make your acquaintance." Mr. Looney speaks like someone from a black-and-white movie; I've sure never heard anyone else talk like this before. He continues, "Atticus here is a fine student, and a fine young man too. Excellent writer, your Atticus."

Excellent writer? What?! We haven't even written anything in English class yet. How does Mr. Looney have any clue what kind of writer I am?

"Thank you for saying that," my mom replies. Then her smile *changes* somehow. I'm not exactly sure what it is, just that it turns real for a second.

I open my car door and climb out of the van.

"Have a good day today, sweetie."

Once I'm outside, I glance back as my mom drives away and, in the rearview mirror, I see her wiping her eyes.

FOURTEEN

THE DEFINITION OF A FATHER

"Atticus, we're starting our first book today." Mr. Looney's voice is as calm as a Cape Cod wave. Even though he must have heard the blowup in our van, he doesn't seem like he even knows about it. Most teachers would have said something like, *What was that all about, Atticus?* or *Why don't we make an appointment for you to see the guidance counselor?*

"What book are we starting?" I ask, happy not to have to talk about the fight in the van.

"It's called *To Kill a Mockingbird*. A woman named Harper Lee wrote it." Mr. Looney opens the door of our English classroom, and he gestures for me to go in before him.

"What's it about?" I ask Mr. Looney as he unloads his bag onto his desk and takes a seat in the old wooden chair.

"It's about two kids who learn life's most important lesson from their father," Mr. Looney says as he stares straight at me. When he pronounces the word *father*, I feel my whole body tense up. I wish I could change the meaning of the word *father.* My mind wanders for a moment as I consider my own possible definitions:

Father (1): A man who is supposed to care about his children but does not.

Father (2): Someone who lies about loving you.

Father (3): Someone who leaves when things get tough.

Mr. Looney continues, "In this book, the father is a kind man but also courageous. In fact, in my humble estimation, the father here is the most heroic man I have ever encountered in my life. Books or otherwise." Mr. Looney looks at me strangely. "Do you want to know what this father's name is, Atticus?"

"Sure," I say, kind of interested.

"Atticus," Mr. Looney says.

"What?"

"Atticus."

"What, Mr. Looney?"

"No, not *you*, but Atticus." Mr. Looney looks at me *really* strangely now.

"What do you mean, *not me, but Atticus*, Mr. Looney?" I'm trying hard to understand what he means, but a flash in my mind says to me, *Maybe the guy is a bit off his rocker. If he is a little crazy, you can't really blame him with all those brain cells dying when you get old.*

"What I mean, my young man, is that the father's name in this book we're going to read—this kind and courageous father—is *Atticus*. His name is the same as yours."

A broad smile stretches across Mr. Looney's face. Then he pats my shoulder. I smile in return, feeling something strange but kind of good in my stomach and chest. A tingling like excitement.

Mr. Looney reaches into his old bag and pulls out a book. "Here's your copy. Why don't you get started a little early? You can stay here in the classroom with me and read the opening pages." Before I reach out for the book, he smells it. I'm not kidding. He *smells* the book. "This copy was mine when I first read it about forty years ago. You can use this one for now."

I take the book from his hands. It's *at least* forty years old. The cover is black and brown, and there's this image of a tree with a black trunk, and its green leaves all fan out like they're reaching for something. I open it up to the first page. Someone has written a note there in thick black ink. Whoever wrote that note also signed a name below it.

"What's this?" I ask.

"It's a note from the author, Harper Lee, along with her signature."

"What does it say?" I can't decipher the awkward, scrawling writing.

"It says: *To Robert: Courage comes when you least expect it—Your friend, Harper Lee.*"

I flip through the pages of the book. Here is my first thought: *Man, the words are tiny, and there are A LOT of pages in this book.*

I usually open a book to check if the chapters are long or short, and somewhere along the way, I've gotten lazy about reading. I loved to read when I was a little kid, but now, whenever we get a new book in school, I can't help groaning. We always have to fill out charts and bubbles and do worksheets and figure out all these right answers that only teachers seem to know.

"My desk is yours, Atticus." Mr. Looney motions for me to sit in the wooden chair at his desk.

I take a seat and begin with chapter one. The opening line of the book goes like this: *When he was nearly thirteen, my brother Jem got his arm badly broken at the elbow.*

FIFTEEN

RUNNING LAPS IN ENGLISH CLASS

When the bell rings to start the school day, I lift my head up from the book for the first time. *Did twenty minutes really go by that fast?* I don't know what it is about this book, or about reading next to Mr. Looney, but it's like I forgot that I was even in stupid Pitts Middle School.

I close the book and stand up.

"Like it so far?" Mr. Looney is sitting at a student desk to my right, writing something.

"Yeah, a lot." I smile at Mr. Looney and walk toward him, holding his book in my outstretched hand.

"You hold onto it for now. Give it back to me once you're all finished." He grins, and then goes back to his writing without so much as saying a *Good-bye* or an *Anything you want to tell me before everyone arrives?*

"Thanks, Mr. Looney."

I put *To Kill a Mockingbird* in my backpack and rush off to my locker.

When it comes time for English class later that morning, Mr. Looney is acting strange again. But then again, strange is Mr. Looney's normal. At the start of class, he's running laps around us in the classroom. A seventy-seven-year-old man *running laps* in our classroom.

Finally, Sam speaks up. "Mr. Looney, what in the world are you doing?" Mr. Looney stops as soon as Sam asks the question.

He looks at Sam and responds, "Thank you, Sam! I thought I was simply going to have to keep running. And, you know, even though I look like I'm in my twenties, I am getting just a bit old." Mr. Looney walks toward the wooden chair at his desk—the same chair where I sat reading *To Kill a Mockingbird* earlier this morning—and sits down. "I was trying to show you something, Sam."

"By running around the classroom?" Sam looks just as bewildered as the rest of us.

"I was trying to show you that if you read a book the way you've been taught to read, you'll end up right where you began. And even though you may be sweating and exhausted, all that reading—like all my running—really hasn't moved you from one place to another. Do you understand what I'm saying to you?"

Sam thinks for a minute, then says, "Not really."

"Let me rephrase, then." Mr. Looney stands up from his wooden chair and walks over to Sam. "What is your name, Sam?"

"What?"

"I said, what is your name, Sam?"

"My name is Sam," Sam replies, looking really confused.

"Good. And what are you afraid of?" Mr. Looney stares right at Sam like he's the only student in the entire classroom.

"Afraid of? Um, I'm afraid of . . . blood. Every time I see it, I get queasy and I feel like I'm just gonna flop right over onto the floor."

"I see," says Mr. Looney. "Well, I'm not afraid of blood at all! In fact, if you really think about it, Sam, there's nothing to be afraid of about blood. It's simply a natural part of your body. I think that only weak people are afraid of seeing a little blood. If you were stronger, you wouldn't be scared of something so natural, don't you think?" Then Mr. Looney looks up at the rest of us.

This is a new side of Mr. Looney. It almost seems like he's trying to make Sam feel stupid. Sam *does* seem to feel stupid too. He shrinks down in his seat, and his face goes all pink.

"*Freeze*! Right there!" Mr. Looney yells as loud as a train wreck.

Sam freezes. I do too. "Right now, Sam, you probably feel a bit foolish. So, forgive me for saying what I said. But I did it to make a point. You shared an honest fear with me, and I proceeded to tell you it was stupid to be afraid of that. I tried to use what *I* already thought to have a conversation with *you*. You were honest, but I wasn't listening. So I didn't get anything out of what you shared with me. I'm in the same place I was before you told me what you were afraid of. I haven't *moved* at all. I think exactly what I thought before, only now I also told you that I thought you were weak and maybe a bit stupid. You follow me?"

Sam looks a little more comfortable. "A little, but I'm still not sure I get it."

"When most teachers and students read a book, they focus on what they *think* is important. They ask questions about the plot and the theme and who did what to whom and when. These teachers and students are missing the big picture. It's like they're telling Sam to simply not be afraid of blood. But there's something so much more important, *so much more important*, when it comes to reading a book."

"What's that?" The words jump out of me before I even think. Surprised to hear my own voice, I sit up. My whole body feels . . . *awake.* Other students are looking at me with surprised eyes.

"Good question, Atticus. The big picture is this: *Who* are the people in the book? Not *what* they're doing—or when or how—but *who* are they? And the even bigger question is this: Who are *you* in *their* company? To be able to answer these questions, you've really got to listen to the souls of the characters, not necessarily just their actions. Like with Sam. I haven't learned anything about Sam if I just tell him that he shouldn't be afraid of blood. I've got to really listen to him, try to see what it feels like to be afraid of what he's afraid of, and then I'm getting somewhere. Then I'm also learning about who I am."

Mr. Looney walks back to his chair. He sits down and looks at us. "And students," he says, "the hardest thing in the world is to really *listen* to another human being without telling them what they should feel or think or do. But if you can't *listen* to the characters in our book, all you'll be doing is running laps—doing the work but never getting anywhere."

I smile. I'm not sure that I get everything Mr. Looney just said. But the pieces that I do understand somehow make me feel stronger in some strange way.

Then Mr. Looney looks at me and says, "Atticus, would you mind holding up the book that we're all going to start reading today?"

At first I feel my legs lock. *Revolt!* they scream. *No standing!* they roar.

But I kind of surprise myself when I hear something inside of me say back, *Shut up!* And then I feel my body rising.

Before I know it, I'm on my feet in English class, Mr. Looney's copy of *To Kill a Mockingbird* in my hand, with a small smile on my face.

Mr. Looney is grinning so big that I wonder if his face can hold it. Then he says, "And Atticus, would you mind sharing with the class what the book is about?"

I keep standing, and with a voice I didn't know I had, I say, "It's about a father named Atticus, and his two kids, and it's about courage."

Even though my heart is pounding, I stand for another moment. Then I risk a glance at Audrey.

She's smiling too.

i GET GLEEFULLY GIDDY IN MATH CLASS

I'm still riding this high from Mr. Looney's class when I get to math that afternoon. It isn't a terrible subject—it was even one of my favorites when I was younger—but our teacher, Mrs. Relton, has so much trouble with Danny that I never feel safe in her classroom. I try to sit as far away from him as possible, but just last week Mrs. Relton put us in a group together.

"Hey, Fatticus. Hey . . . Dwarf-boy!" Danny's yelling at me in whispers. Mrs. Relton is at the front of the class drawing x and y coordinates on a graph. I pretend not to hear Danny and continue copying down the coordinates as Mrs. Relton puts them on the board. But Danny isn't letting this one go. *"Hey, Fatticus!"*

I look at Danny and say, "What?"

I want to be angry. I want to look at Danny and say, *What, Moron?!* But all I can muster is the squeak of a mouse.

"How did that dirt taste on Saturday? You hungry for more, Fatticus? Maybe next time you want some worms mixed in there for extra flavoring?"

I look at him quickly, then my eyes drop to my open binder and notes. Danny hasn't even taken out his binder, let alone paper. I mean, he isn't even *pretending* to follow Mrs. Relton as she goes through her lesson. Every second that ticks past makes me more furious. I'm SICK and TIRED of feeling like there's nothing I can do.

I'M SICK OF BEING A WUSS.

I think of how I wanted to scream when Danny knocked me to the ground and beat me up. I think of how my dad just left us. Then I think of Mr. Looney and those steady green eyes—not flinching for anything.

I look up from my binder and glare at Danny. And I don't know where the words come from—only that they are loud.

"Shut up!"

They fly from my mouth like they've been there for years, caged up and waiting for someone to open the door and let them go.

Danny slides back in his chair, and then he almost tips over onto the floor. I'm not kidding. He catches his chair in time and looks at me like he can't believe it's *me*. Everyone in the class, including Audrey, turns toward us.

"Atticus, what's this all about?" Mrs. Relton's face is red and confused.

"I don't know." As I answer Mrs. Relton, I can feel this big smile spreading across me *everywhere*, like my whole body is a mouth and even then it can't fit the smile.

"What do you mean, you don't know? How can you not know what this is about? You just yelled *shut up* in the middle of my class. You *have* to know what this is about."

"I'm sorry, Mrs. Relton, but I can't even explain it." I feel excited and happy and nervous all at the same time. And all

I can think is, *So this is what it feels like to use my voice in class*.

"Atticus, go to the principal's office, okay? Tell them what happened, and we'll deal with this later."

I stand up and head for the door of the classroom. But just before I leave the room, I turn around and look right back at Danny and say as loudly as I can, "And don't let it happen again!"

I stay in the room long enough to see Danny's furious scowl but not long enough for Mrs. Relton to heap more punishments on my head.

As I open the classroom door, it's like I don't care that Danny is going to pummel me even harder than he did before. All I care about, in this instant, is one thing: I don't want to be afraid anymore.

SEVENTEEN

BIG BROWN EYES

In the hallway, as I am walking toward Mr. Callahan's office, my head still buzzes from the feeling of my own voice—loud enough for Danny, Mrs. Relton, and *everyone in class* to hear. Then a voice catches me.

"Atticus! Atticus, wait up."

It's Audrey.

She's got her blue backpack on one arm, her math textbook and binder in the other, trying to put everything together as she hurries toward me. In a flash, my voice disappears and I feel dizzy.

"Atticus, hold on a minute." Audrey finally catches up to where I'm now frozen to the floor of the school hallway. "What was Danny doing this time?" Audrey looks up at me with these big brown eyes—I mean, she *looks* at me. Here's the most beautiful girl in the world and she even FOLLOWED ME OUT OF THE CLASSROOM TO CATCH ME.

"Uh . . . um . . . I mean . . . nothing." What I'm thinking about as her big brown eyes search my face is not what just happened in math class with Danny. Nothing could be *further* from my mind right now.

Here's what I *am* thinking: *Audrey Higgins is talking to me in the middle of the hallway. She's looking at me with those big, beautiful brown eyes. Those brown eyes that could swallow me right up. I could dive into those eyes and swim faster than any world-record holder ever has. Atticus, pinch yourself to make sure this is really happening. No, don't pinch yourself. Because, if this is really happening, and you go and do something stupid like pinching yourself in the middle of the school hallway while Audrey Higgins (Audrey Higgins!) is talking to you, then she might think you're a little strange and stop talking to you. Okay, new plan: don't pinch yourself. But those eyes! Just remember those eyes. Hold on to those eyes, and no matter what other kinds of crap you have to deal with . . .*

But Audrey doesn't give up on figuring out what really happened in math class with Danny. So here's how the rest of the conversation goes:

Audrey: "Atticus, what *was* Danny doing this time? Tell me, I'll believe you."

My Mind: *She said my name! Audrey Higgins said my name! And man, did you hear the way she said my name? I mean, she didn't just say it like she was asking someone to pass the ketchup or something. NO, she said it like she meant it—like she really meant it!*

Me: "What . . . uh . . . what's that?"

Audrey: "Atticus, are you okay?"

My Mind: *She cares about me, man! Audrey Higgins wants to know if I am okay. Audrey Higgins! But don't even get into the pinching stuff again, man—this is real. You are here, Audrey Higgins is here, and now just answer the question. Are you okay, Atticus? Atticus! Answer those big, beautiful, brown eyes. Are you okay?*

Me: "I've never been better, Audrey."

I enter the main office of the school with even my feet tingling. My face is wide with a smile that feels monstrous—the way you feel when you've just come home from the dentist and your cheeks are pumped full of Novocain and feel ten times their normal size.

The secretary, Mrs. James, notices it.

"Well, Atticus, it's not every day we see a smile on your face." She looks up after hanging up the phone.

"Hi, Mrs. James. I'm supposed to come see Mr. Callahan. Mrs. Relton sent me." I want to get in quick and see the principal while I'm still riding my high of standing up to Danny (well, *kind of* standing up to Danny) and speaking with Audrey in the hallway (well, *kind of* speaking with Audrey).

"Oh, I'm sorry, Atticus. Mr. Callahan is currently in a meeting with some members of the school board. It's one of those long ones, you know?" Then she smiles.

I don't know, maybe God is smiling on me right at that moment. Or maybe the Man Upstairs is just thinking, *You know what? Atticus has had it pretty hard lately. I'm gonna throw an easy pitch his way. Just this once . . .* Because Mrs. James looks at me and says, "Tell you what, Atticus, why don't you sit by my desk for a bit—and then I'll send you to your next period once the bell rings? Mrs. Relton doesn't have to know Mr. Callahan was in a meeting, right?"

And I shake my head from side to side, the happiness unable to squeeze into words.

◉ ◉ ◉

That night, my mom makes chili. Adrian and I sit at the dinner table. He makes farting noises by putting his mouth to the corner of the table. I don't know how he does it, but he manages to get a loud sound from the table that would have made you believe you'd really heard someone rip a big one.

Then he starts singing, "Beans, beans, they make you fart, the more you eat, the more you fart! The more you fart, the more you fart! So eat your beans with every meal!"

I start in on him. "Adrian, that's not even how the song goes, you only—"

"Is too!" he interrupts me.

"No, it's not!" I yell back.

I realize, then, that I'm arguing with my six-year-old brother over how a song about beans and farting goes. So I smile.

Just as my mom carries over two steaming bowls of beans and meat, the smile turns into a laugh. Me laughing makes Adrian laugh. Then my mom seems to catch the vibe, and she starts laughing too.

Before I know it, the three of us are laughing right there at the kitchen table, our bowls of steaming chili in front of us. Adrian stops laughing every once in a while to make an ever-more-intense farting sound on the corner of the table. This only makes my mom and me laugh more.

It's the first time we laugh since my dad left.

Even though our chili meal was pretty awesome, when the weekend comes, my mom is really quiet, and the pretend smile shows up again and again. Friday night we order pizza. And Saturday we order pizza again.

My mom isn't doing a lot of the stuff she normally does. In the laundry room, the pile of dirty clothes is enormous. Usually, she washes all of our clothes and has them folded and in our drawers every morning—like the Santa Claus of Clean Laundry. But there have been a lot of mornings with no clean clothes lately.

The dishes too. Our kitchen sink is pretty big, but now it looks tiny since the collection of crusty cereal bowls and other dirty dishes fill it completely. More food-stuck dishes are even piled on the counter near the sink because they can't fit inside it.

And the garage. Soon after my dad left, I noticed that my mom started moving anything that belonged to Dad—even anything he *used*—into the garage. The van can't even fit inside the garage anymore.

After I finish the pizza, I go out into the garage to see if there are any new additions to the clutter there. The piles are huge. And my mom definitely didn't take any special care in dumping the stuff.

I see picture frames with our whole family, smashed against some boxes. I see my dad's workout bench and most of his weights in a pile (she must not have been able to carry the really heavy weights out to the garage). I see a bunch of my dad's shirts and ties—ones he must have left home, thinking maybe he'd come back for them?

The most interesting thing I find, though, is a couple of shoeboxes full of papers. Inside are all these letters my mom and dad wrote each other when they were a whole lot younger. It must have been years ago, before I was born, because the way they wrote each another is like nothing I've *ever* heard them say in my lifetime.

I open one of the shoeboxes—a red and white box that says "Penny Loafers" on the side—and pull out the letter on top. It says:

Dear Helen,

It's hard to believe that only two months have passed since we first met by the water fountain in the park. Remember? You were eating that ice cream cone that was dripping all over you, and when I came over to ask you for directions, you looked up at me and your face was covered in straw-berry ice cream. Then you just broke out laughing.

Ever since I heard that laugh, I knew I wanted to spend the rest of my life with you. You'll be a painter, and I'll be a writer—and we'll both chase down our dreams together. Forever.

Forever!

All My Love,

James

I can't believe it. Was this *really* my father? If so, what aliens abducted him and gave me the dud instead? Where is this guy who wrote that he would stick around forever?

I reread that letter three more times. I keep focusing on the line about him and my mom being a writer and a painter. *A writer and a painter?* The only jobs I ever saw my parents work were as a secretary (my mom) and an insurance agent (my dad). I never saw a single painting my mom did or a single story my dad wrote.

I pull out the next letter. It's from my mom to my dad. Before I even open it up, I notice that it has all these tiny red hearts all over the envelope. And on the seal, it looks like she had put on lipstick and then kissed it. My mom's letter goes like this:

Dear James,

I simply cannot wait until you move here to Windsor. I know my dad isn't too happy about us getting married this soon. But what does he know? I don't think anyone can really understand how much we love one another. When I am with you, I feel as though I can paint the entire sky full of stars and still not capture how beautiful and peaceful it feels when we're together.

Let's save these letters, and one day, when we're old and our children have moved on to bigger and better things, we'll take them out of some closet and read them together, giggling at how in love we were. And, what's better, we'll still be madly in love when we read them so many years later!

I love you with all my heart and soul, and I can't wait to see you this weekend so that we can start planning our wedding. And our lives together!

Love and Kisses (Lots of Kisses!),

Helen

Around her name, at the bottom of the letter, she drew a big heart and colored all of it red except the part where her name was written.

How can two people who seemed to love each other so much end up fighting constantly and then get separated? It just doesn't make any kind of sense to me.

And even though I still hate my father, the words he wrote in his letter make me think about how much he once loved my mom. My dad has obviously changed his mind. But I don't think my mom has.

My mom.

She really does do all the work in the house, and she's constantly telling me that she loves me (sometimes I have to ask her *not* to tell me she loves me so often). My mom just seems to give and give and give. And whoever gives back to her?

As I sit on the floor in the garage with those shoeboxes full of letters, two ideas hit me. I hurry back upstairs. There isn't much time left in the night.

EIGHTEEN

i BATTLE THE WASHING MACHINE

I've never done laundry before. Maybe that's a little ridiculous. But my mom just takes care of all that stuff, so I've never taken the time to learn. But tonight, I want to *give* something to my mom, and laundry is what comes to mind first.

So I load all the clothes from the hamper into the washer, stuffing in more and more dirty laundry until the machine is crammed as full as I can get it. I find a big blue bottle of liquid soap with the word PUREX on the side. I pick up the bottle and pour a bunch of soap in. I know these dirty clothes have been sitting here for a while, so I figure a ton of soap ought to help. I push the lid down until I hear a click and then look at all the options on the big round dial and the buttons in front of me.

> Whites
> Casuals
> Heavy
> Medium
> Light
> Rinse & Spin

Huh? I crammed in a lot of clothes that were white, but some of them were bright red or blue. Also I put a lot of casual clothes in, but there were a lot of my mom's business suits for her job as a secretary—definitely *not* casual. And what's the deal with the *heavy, medium,* and *light* options? Most of the clothes weigh about the same, and I don't know if that's heavier or lighter than normal. And the whole *rinse & spin* thing?

But I really don't want to ask my mom how to do it. So I just push all three of the *Heavy, Medium,* and *Light* buttons at once and figure whichever one stays depressed is a good choice. The *Medium* button stays down. Good. Then I point the dial arrow right smack in the middle of *Casuals* and *Whites* (since there are some of both in there).

Nothing happens.

I push and pull the machine back and forth.

Zip.

I yell at the washing machine.

Then I look across the dashboard of the machine. There's no *On* button. There's no switch to flip, like on the TV. I stare at the washing machine for a long time. It's a showdown, and one of us is going to walk away the loser.

And you'd better believe I am *not* going to lose to a hunk of metal and knobs. My Imagination takes over, and the battle goes like this:

Washing Machine: *Good luck, Fatticus! Ha! You don't have the slightest clue how to operate me, do you? You've got nothing, buddy. Nothing!*

Me: *Oh, really? You think I've got nothing? I've got arms and legs and I can talk, but what can you do? You sit there and shake back and forth with a bunch of water and soap. How's that for nothing?*

Washing Machine: *Oh, so you're going to make yourself feel better by making fun of my lack of arms and legs, are you? Go ahead if it makes you feel better about yourself, but it still isn't going to get you one bit closer to beating me at my own game. And I'm not saying a word—you hear me . . . Not a word!*

Me: *I'm not asking you to tell me a single thing. I wouldn't want to beat you that way. I'm going to win this battle fair and square. I'm going to figure you out and take you down.*

Washing Machine: *You're not taking anything down!*

Me: *Am too!*

Washing Machine: *Are not!*

Me: *Fart-face!*

Washing Machine: *Dwarf-boy!*

Me: *Fart-face!*

Washing Machine: *Dwarf-boy!*

Just when I think all is lost—as I am becoming my little brother and the washing machine is becoming Danny—I lunge for the circular knob and pull it, thinking I'll just rip the stupid knob right off the machine. Instead, the button pops out and the machine starts to hum. Opening the lid, I'm amazed to see a heavy stream of water rush into the top of the machine.

I win.

i TRY MY HAND AT A LOVE LETTER

My second idea of the night is to write a love letter to Audrey. Call me silly. Call me stupid. Call me whatever you like, but reading those notes from my parents did something to me. It's not like I changed my whole perspective on life or anything. But I get it now—that my mom thought she was going to be with my dad forever. Whatever reasons my dad had for leaving, they don't cut it with me. It wasn't wrong that my dad wrote those things—it was just wrong that he didn't follow through on them. He wrote *forever*, and then he left before forever had ended.

But I can be different from him. I can write a note like that and then follow through on it. If I write *forever*, I'm going to mean it. I'm not going to be my dad.

I sit down at my desk, pull out my binder, and grab a piece of paper. Then I realize that I might not get my love letter right the first time. (It is my first love letter ever, after all.) So I take out four more sheets of paper. *Just in case.*

I take a deep breath, hold the blue pen in my hand, and start writing. My first attempt comes out like this:

Dear Audrey,

Your brown eyes are so brown and beautiful. When you stopped me in the hallway after Mrs. Relton made me leave math class the other day, it was awesome. I love talking to you. I love the way you talk, and your ideas, and the way you look. And I love that you are so kind to everybody, no matter how popular they are. Not many people in our school are like that. But you are, and I think it's really, really cool.

Anyway, I wondered if you would want to go out with me. I mean, not out anywhere in particular (although, of course, we could go out to particular places if you wanted to . . . in fact, that would be awesome if you wanted to go out to particular places . . . I'm just saying we wouldn't HAVE to). So, if you want to be my girlfriend, I would be so excited that I'd have a permanent smile across my face for . . . forever.

Sincerely,

Atticus Hobart
(from math and English class)

I look at the letter I just wrote. It just poured out of me. As I reread it, I can see it's not a *terrible* letter. But then again, it's no masterpiece. I can't help thinking that I sound like a little kid. And I want to sound mature, smart, wise, romantic. So I hold the sheet of paper up in front of me and do something I haven't done in a long, long time—something I detest.

I revise my writing.

I start with my first line. I've paid enough attention in English classes to know that the first line—*the hook,* teachers always call it—has to be the best line in the whole thing. I reread my first line out loud: *Your brown eyes are so brown and beautiful.* Did I really write that? Was I really going to tell Audrey Higgins that her brown eyes are brown? I sound like a complete moron. That's like saying to someone, *Oh, yeah, that salt is salty* or *Oh, yeah, that green tree over there is green.*

I change the first line to read: *Your brown eyes are beautiful to me.* I think the last words *to me* are a nice touch, and now the line feels strong and sweet.

I move on to my second line: *When you stopped me in the hallway after Mrs. Relton made me leave math class the other day, it was awesome.* It seems like I used the word *awesome* because I didn't know what I really wanted to say.

So I sit at my desk and try to answer the tough question: *What was awesome about it?* I start to brainstorm ideas: It was awesome because I got to look at her for a long time . . . it was awesome because I felt all tingly inside while we talked in the hallway . . . it was awesome because I felt safe with her, like we were *supposed* to be there talking with each other.

Aha! That's it. *Safety.* I rewrite the second line so that it now reads: *The other day, when you stopped me in the hallway, I felt this strange safety as we talked, and I don't normally feel that way at school.*

Now, since I'm building up some steam for this revising thing, I plunge right on into my third line: *I love talking to you.* Actually, that isn't half bad. I decide to leave that one alone.

My fourth line says: *I love the way you talk, and your ideas, and the way you look.* I realize that sentence is basically unnecessary. It doesn't really do that much for the note. So I draw a thick line right through it and move on to my fifth line: *And I love that you are so kind to everybody, no matter how popular they are.* The cool thing about the fifth line, I now realize, is that it flows really nicely from the third line, so I leave this one alone too and move on to my next line: *Not many people in our school are like that*. It's true, I realize, and decide to leave that one alone as well.

I ditch the next line because saying that something is *really, really cool* doesn't seem all that necessary when you've already told someone that you love the way they are.

I take a deep breath. I'm making a lot of progress. I re-read my second paragraph, though, and feel overwhelmed. It doesn't make any sense—I just rambled on and on and on and on.

So I ask myself another question: *What do you really want to know, Atticus?* And I already have the answer. *I want to know if Audrey will be my girlfriend.* So, I decide to be honest and just write that.

Now that my revision is complete, I rewrite the new note on a separate sheet of paper. It goes like this:

Dear Audrey,

Your brown eyes are beautiful to me. The other day, when you stopped me in the hallway, I felt this strange safety as we talked, and I don't normally feel that way at school. I love talking to you. And I love that you are so kind to everybody, no matter how popular they are. Not many people in our school are like that.

So, to be completely honest, I was wondering if you would be my girlfriend.

Sincerely,

Atticus Hobart

I look at the page and resist a sudden urge to draw a heart around my name, like my mom did in her letter so long ago. Instead, I fold it and put it into my top desk drawer.

Tomorrow, if I can work up the courage, I'll give it to Audrey and see what turn my life takes next.

◎ ◎ ◎

Just before I fall asleep that night, my mom rushes into my bedroom.

"Atticus, did you put those clothes in the washer?" Her voice is loud and really emotional. *Great*, I think, *a really good day is about to get screwed up with an argument because I tried to do something nice and messed up.*

I nod.

Just as I'm getting ready for my mom to let me have it, she starts crying. And when I say crying, I mean *crying*. Her shoulders rise and fall in great big heaves as she lets out these huge sobs.

"Mom. Mom! What happened? What's wrong?" I feel the panic inside me rising.

Finally, my mom takes a deep breath, collects herself, and looks right at me. "No. Nothing at all is wrong, honey. Everything is wonderful . . . so, so wonderful." And then she walks over to me, puts her arms around me, and gives me the kind of bear hug you only get when you're four years old and you say something adorable.

Then she holds me away from her just a bit and stares full into my face. She wipes her eyes. "Have I told you how much I love you, Atticus?"

And then I get it.

I hug my mom back—for the first time in a long time— and say quickly, "Love you too, Mom.

TWENTY

MY LAST BASEBALL GAME

This is my last baseball game. Not because the season is over, but because I've decided to quit the team. I don't like baseball. Never really did. But since it was the only thing my dad ever really wanted to do with me, I kept at it, thinking it'd make him keep loving me.

But now that my dad is not even here anymore, why stay? My mom told me it would be respectful to go to the game today, play through it, and then tell Coach Wills at the end.

It's the bottom of the fourth inning, and I've already gotten two strikeouts. Danny is worse than ever—calling me names loud enough for the whole team, and *especially* his dad, Coach Wills, to hear. But no one cares.

In fact, Coach Wills doesn't seem to care about anything at all today. Even when I strike out, he doesn't grumble like normal. Plus he kind of staggers around the dugout, looking at all of us with these weird eyes.

Danny grabs the bat and makes his way toward the on-deck box. But before he gets there, Coach yells, "Hey! Get your butt over here!"

Coach Wills has said a lot of mean things, but it's the first time I've heard him yell anything negative to Danny. While I'm trying to figure out what's going on, something else grabs my attention.

Danny's face is growing redder by the second, and he starts kicking his bat as he looks down at the dirt. Finally, he looks up.

"Dad—no." He turns around and walks away from his father.

"I said, *get . . . your . . . lazy butt . . . over here.*" Coach Wills kind of stumbles out of the dugout and onto the side of the field. He grabs Danny's uniform and tries to pull him back, but he can't quite hold onto it.

Danny runs towards the on-deck box; Coach walks back inside the dugout.

The ump comes over to the dugout and says quietly, "Coach, can I see you for a minute?"

"Leave me alone, dang it." Coach Wills won't look up at the ump. Instead, he comes toward me, of all people. He sits down on the end of the bench, right beside me. And now I know what's going on. I can *smell* it. The stuff is strong, and I can tell that Danny's dad has had too much to drink.

The ump comes farther into the dugout. "Listen, Bill, you can either come with me now and I'll call Cheryl and we all keep this real quiet, or we get a whole bunch of parents up in arms and you'll have a lot of explaining to do." The ump nods his head toward the dugout's exit.

Coach Wills gets up and walks beside the ump.

I stand up too and follow Coach along the length of the dugout. As he leaves, I watch him closely. When he passes Danny, I hear Coach say, "Worthless." It's quiet, but I hear it.

The ump yells out for everyone to hear, "Coach Wills is pretty sick—must have that flu virus that's going around. I'll get him settled, and then we'll play out the inning."

When Danny looks back toward the dugout, his eyes meet mine. Even though I still hate him, I can also feel my eyes saying something else to Danny—something like, *I'm sorry about your dad.*

I don't know why.

But then I see what Danny's eyes say back to me: *You're going to get it.* He lifts the bat above his shoulders and tightens his grip around the handle.

Even though it makes absolutely no sense at all, I get it. In some weird way, I understand why he's going to come after me. I just have to figure out how to stop it.

In our last at-bats of the inning, Danny strikes out.

I strike out too, but on the last pitch of the game—and maybe of my life—I get a foul tip. I swing hard, and I hear the *clink* of the ball off my bat. Just a foul tip, which only aids my way to a strikeout. But my bat connects with a pitch—I make contact.

And it feels like a home run.

TWENTY-ONE

ALMOST THE WORST HOMEWORK ASSIGNMENT IN THE HISTORY OF HOMEWORK ASSIGNMENTS

It's our third week with Mr. Looney, and so far he hasn't given us a single homework assignment. We did a conga line in class, we roared like lions, we did some serious eye-staring, and we watched Mr. Looney run laps around the classroom. But no homework.

Until today.

"What do you think of when you hear the word *homework*?" Mr. Looney asks us. He's walking around the outside of the circle of desks. Almost every day he arranges the desks in some new way. Today, it's a huge circle.

For a while, no one responds. Then Sam yells out, "I think of worksheets. Awful worksheets with a tiny space for my name and a bunch of blanks."

Mr. Looney doesn't say anything except, "Hhhmm."

By now I've gotten used to these kinds of sounds coming from him. No matter what any of us says, Mr. Looney *actually* thinks about it, as if he's flipping our words around in his brain like a pancake, seeing how cooked both sides are, and letting us know that no matter what we say, we've got a point.

Then Mr. Looney laughs and says, "I'd rather be tied to a rock and have a vulture peck my eyeballs out over and over for all eternity than do a single worksheet."

My own laughter bursts out of me. The rest of the class is laughing too, even clapping hands and hollering a little as well.

When things calm down, Margaret says, "But you're a teacher! Aren't you kind of responsible for even *making up* the idea of worksheets?"

Mr. Looney looks at her, and he breaks into a big smile. He walks toward her desk and says, "It's a good question, Margaret." Then he walks away, into the center of the circle of our desks.

He looks around at all of us like he knows some huge secret that we don't know. I don't even realize it for a moment, but when my butt starts to hurt, I finally notice that I've been sliding forward, sitting on the edge of my seat.

When he speaks, his voice is loud and excited. "Students, did you know that there is a certain type of rhinoceros that lives in Africa that excretes its entire body weight every forty-eight hours?"

I burst out laughing again. Audrey and a few others do too.

But Sam shouts out, "Mr. Looney, what is *excretes*?"

Mr. Looney smiles real wide now and replies, "Poop, Sam. Excrement. Waste. Unnecessary materials. Food that has packed its bags and is ready to board the plane!" He's on a roll now, and the entire class is laughing. I don't know why, but I glance over at Danny. His hat is pulled over his head, and I can't see his eyes.

"So, then, what am I saying here, class? Anyone want to rephrase for me?" Mr. Looney looks right where I just did.

"Danny, how about it? What am I really saying here?" Danny pulls his cap down farther. Then Mr. Looney asks Hannah.

Hannah replies, "You're saying that there's a kind of rhinoceros that poops its whole body weight every two days." She laughs in between the words.

"Precisely!" Mr. Looney actually jumps off the ground. "So just because one *type* of rhinoceros produces more poop than you would ever want to see in your life, it doesn't mean *all* rhinoceroses do as well, right? Atticus?"

I feel my heart speed up at the mention of my name. But I take a breath and reply with the strongest voice I have, "You're making an analogy, Mr. Looney. Some teachers are like those rhinoceroses, and some are . . . *different*." I pause for a moment, and the class feels so still, so safe. "You're different."

"Precisely!" Mr. Looney smiles and walks back outside the circle and sits in his chair, right next to me. Then he swivels around like a bolt of lightning and says, "What do you think, Margaret? Satisfied that I in no way corroborated with the conception of worksheets as a meaningful endeavor?"

Margaret laughs. I do too.

"So, then, allow me to introduce your first homework assignment by saying that it is most definitely *not* a worksheet." I don't know exactly how he does it, but I can feel myself getting *excited* about the homework he's about to assign. "Here is your real homework assignment. Are you ready?"

And at these three words, we all pull out our journals. Last week, Mr. Looney gave each of us a big, bound book filled with blank paper. He said we'd use these for everything—writing, thoughts, poems, homework, *everything*. And for half a class we practiced whipping them out when he said the words: *Are you ready?* We had competitions about who could do it fastest, and he even made a huge ARE YOU READY? tournament bracket on the board to record the results. (Audrey won.)

With our journals open in front of us, Mr. Looney goes on, "It's one single question that you have to ask one of your parents. That's it. Just write down this one question, ask one of your parents tonight, and then write everything they say back to you—no matter how short or long it is."

He gets up from his wooden chair and goes to the whiteboard. After picking up a dry-erase marker, he writes in cursive: *What scares you most about yourself?*

As soon as he writes the question, my hand freezes. Suddenly, I can't tell whether this will be the easiest or the absolute hardest homework assignment of my life.

Then, something inside me says, *Depends on which parent you ask, Atticus.*

◎ ◎ ◎

That night, after dinner, I get up the courage to ask my mom. "Do you have Dad's cell number?"

My question kind of floors her. I can tell because she stops drying the dishes and turns and looks straight at me with eyes that look confused and even a little hurt.

"Are you sure you want it, Atticus?"

I think for another moment. Why do I want to ask my dad, anyway? It would be a lot easier just to ask my mom, write down her response, and be done with it all. But there's this other voice in me—telling me that I've *got* to ask my dad because that's who I'm afraid to ask.

"I'm sure, Mom." I smile at her, wanting to let her know that it'll be okay.

She gives me the number, and I call from my bedroom.

After the fourth ring, I think he's not going to answer. I feel my body relax. I won't have to do this after all, and it won't be because I was afraid.

But as if the phone itself heard my thoughts, I hear a click and then my Dad's voice. "Helen?"

"No, it's me." I try to sound as calm as I can, but as soon as I hear his voice, all I want to do is scream at him.

"Oh, hi, Sport. I mean—Atticus. How have you been?" My dad sounds nervous, and I can already imagine him sitting there, wishing he wasn't on the phone with me right now.

"Do you really care? At all?" My voice is getting louder, and I like the way it feels.

"Care about what?"

"What do you mean, about what? Do you really care about how I'm doing?!" It doesn't come out as a question—not even close.

For a moment my dad is quiet, and I wonder if he's going to just hang up and continue to pretend he doesn't have any sons.

Instead, his voice comes back softer. "Look, I don't know, okay? There's a lot I don't know right now. That's it. I just don't know what I think anymore."

I feel my anger calm down a little, and I know it's time to ask the question I need to ask; because Mr. Looney's question is *my* question too.

"What scares you most about yourself?" I hear my voice stretch itself out like a long rubber band, and I can feel the pressure of the words trying to crack it.

Then, for a long time, the line is dead. Eventually, I hear his breath coming fast. And faster.

"Dad?" No reply. Just faster and faster breathing. And then it catches. I hear him suck in the air so fast that I know exactly what's happening.

He's crying.

I hold the phone so tightly to my face that my ear stings. I've heard my dad scream at me or Adrian, and at my mom, and I've seen his disgusted, I'm-so-ashamed-of-you look while I tried to hit a home run.

But I've never heard him cry.

After what feels like a long time, I hear his breathing slow, and he finally responds with one word. A single word.

"Everything."

Without saying good-bye, I hang up the phone. I'm not sure I really understand what he means by it, but I feel like I could cry too. I write the word in my journal, right underneath the question that I copied down from the board earlier today.

EVERYTHING.

And then, while I'm staring hard at the single word my dad gave me as a reply, I finally get one clear thought in my head: *It's not about me. My dad leaving us really isn't about me or Adrian or even my mom.*

I don't know why, but somehow repeating that thought over and over to myself as I'm lying in bed that night helps me fall asleep. It's a thick blanket I pull over myself, and it keeps me warm in a way I had forgotten how to feel.

TWENTY-TWO

ARE WE REALLY ALL ICEBERGS?

I still haven't given the love note to Audrey. Every day before school, I take it out of the top desk drawer at my house and swear, *Today, I will definitely give Audrey the note*. But as each school day passes and I see Audrey in math and English class, I just can't work up the courage to give it to her.

So it becomes a routine to put the note in my left jeans pocket each morning before I leave home, then to take it out of the same pocket each day after school, and put it back inside my desk drawer safely for the night.

In English class we're still reading Harper Lee's book, *To Kill a Mockingbird*, and I love every second of it. I know that's a strange thing to say—that I love a book, *and* that I love a book *during* school. But I do.

Ever since that early morning when I went into Mr. Looney's class to read, I've kept up the trend. I get to school about thirty minutes early, carrying Mr. Looney's autographed copy of *To Kill a Mockingbird*. I sit on his wooden chair and read while he writes next to me.

Just being in his company feels safe somehow. Like the world can't really hurt me. Sometimes Mr. Looney asks me questions about the book. Sometimes he asks me questions about my life. And I don't feel scared to answer him. It's weird, but I tell him everything. I tell him about my father and how he just left one day. I tell him about Danny Wills. I tell him about Coach Wills. And he always looks right at me with his big, green eyes, nods his head every once in a while, and says, "I see, Son. I see."

And that's all. He doesn't tell me what to do or how to make it better or why I shouldn't feel all the junk I'm feeling. He just keeps saying, "I see, Son. I see." And then he asks another question, or I go back to reading about Atticus.

I've been talking more with Audrey as well, and going to school every day feels—and I'm not kidding here—exciting. Knowing that I'm going to see Mr. Looney and Audrey every day changes everything. At home, too, my mom even seems a little better. Her eyes are not as red and raw. Adrian also seems okay. I don't know what's going to happen with my dad, but I do have this weird feeling like things are making sense. Somehow, my life is making more sense to me than it has in a long time.

But there *are* two big things I can't quite figure out, no matter how long or how hard I try: *Why hasn't Danny gotten back at me for me telling him to shut up during math class a couple of weeks ago?* and *What is going on with Danny's dad?*

Freezing. Absolutely freezing.

"What's going on in here?" Sam asks as we all find our seats and begin shivering. Mr. Looney's classroom feels about as cold as the North Pole, and when I breathe, puffs of steam exit my mouth and swirl, then disappear, in the space in front of my face.

This is crazy. I know Mr. Looney has done some weird stuff (okay—*really* weird stuff) since we've had him over the past six weeks. But making the classroom into Antarctica?! Seriously?

At the front of the room, Mr. Looney is wearing a massive wool hat. It has these big brown flaps that cover his ears, and it reaches about ten feet up toward the ceiling. He's also wearing snowpants, so when he walks towards us, they make the *swish-swash* sound every time he takes a stride.

"Welcome to your real life!" Mr. Looney yells out.

I look over at Audrey, and she is smiling like this is the best thing ever. I risk a glance at Danny, and he's got his hat pulled down over his face, sitting totally still.

"These are the conditions under which we all live and move and relate to one another. Right?" Mr. Looney *swish-swashes* around the first row of desks and then *swish-swashes* down the second row, looking at each of us in the eyes as he walks.

Hannah blurts out, "No way, Mr. Looney! I mean, when winter comes, I stay inside by the fire and under about a thousand blankets on my bed. Nothing like this!"

"Ah, I see, Hannah. But even when you are by the fire, and even when you are under a trillion of the thickest blankets ever made by humankind, you still live in conditions like these." Mr. Looney stops *swish-swashing* and gestures with his arms to encompass the entire classroom.

All I can think is, *how did he even get this room to be so cold?*

"Right?" Mr. Looney asks.

Swish-swash, swish-swash, swish-swash.

"No . . . I mean . . . what do you mean, Mr. Looney?" Sam says what we're all thinking.

"Let me show you," Mr. Looney replies, then hits a button on the projector. All of a sudden, this huge picture of an iceberg flashes onto the whiteboard. This thing is *massive*. It looks like a mountain of ice above the surface of deep, dark blue water. But the crazy thing is, pretty much the whole iceberg is *under* the water. It's like whoever took the picture was able to capture not just the part of the iceberg that sticks up above the surface, but the whole thing.

"What do you notice, class?" Mr. Looney asks.

Swish-swash, swish-swash, swish-swash.

No one says anything. The classroom is seriously colder than our freezer at home, and my skin begins to grow goose bumps.

Then Mr. Looney hits the lights, and the whole room is now dark *and* freezing. So the only thing we can see is this shining blue image with the white iceberg poking its head out above the ocean water.

I suddenly feel safe—safer than I have ever felt at school. Why the darkness and the cold make me feel somehow warm, I don't know. But the light inside my head shoots itself to my throat and I say, "Most of the iceberg is all below the surface of the ocean, Mr. Looney. In fact, seems like pretty much all of it is below the surface. And it's huge—bigger than I ever would have guessed an iceberg could be."

With my words, the goose bumps fade and a tingling replaces them—something like . . . confidence, almost. Like I want to keep talking, keep feeling warm.

"And if I say that you are an iceberg, Atticus—and you too, Sam, and you as well, Audrey and Hannah and Danny and—if I say *all of you are icebergs*, what do you think I mean by that?"

Swish-swash, swish-swash. Mr. Looney stands in front of the projector so that his shadow partially covers the image of the iceberg, and it almost looks like he's holding it when he raises his hands.

And the words are there. I just know them before I even think them. "It means that what really makes me *me* is hard to see just by looking at me. Who I really am is below the surface, and anyone who looks at the tiny part of me that pokes above the surface, well, they're not seeing me. They're not seeing me at all."

I can feel my lips vibrating. I wonder if Danny has heard these words. I wonder if Audrey has heard these words.

Swish-swash, swish-swash, swish-swash.

The lights flash back on, and Mr. Looney says, "*Feel* it, class. *See* it. *Hear* what Atticus just told us. There is so much more to all of us than we see. So much of our pain, our joy, our hope, and our fear rests beneath the surface of what we show to others. We are icebergs, class. Every single one of us. And before you judge a person or a character or *yourself*, remember that there's a whole lot more below the surface you might not know, a whole lot more you might not be seeing."

The whole rest of the day, my lips keep feeling like they're vibrating. And the chill that began in Mr. Looney's classroom becomes like a fire inside of me. I feel—somehow—both small and big at the same time. I feel hot and cold at the same time. More than anything, though, I feel *alive* all at once.

TWENTY-THREE

WALLS

"Personally, Atticus is a dumb ass if you ask me." It's the first time Danny has raised his hand in Mr. Looney's English class to say anything in a class discussion—even though Mr. Looney has been teaching us for almost two months now.

I stare at Mr. Looney, wondering what he's going to say about Danny swearing in class. And I have to admit that my heart starts pounding when Danny says my name—even though he's not talking about *me*; he's talking about the character Atticus Finch.

"Hhhmm, is that so, Daniel?" I have never heard anyone call Danny by his full name in school.

"Yeah, that's so, Old Man. Atticus equals *dumb ass*." Danny leans back in his chair.

"Technically, Daniel, you are a dumb ass as well." Mr. Looney pauses and looks straight at Danny. I can't help wondering if my Imagination just leapt into control of my brain.

Did Mr. Looney really just call Danny Wills a dumb ass in front of the entire class? But when I look around at all the other students, their faces show me it's real.

"See, Daniel, the word *dumb* actually means *unable to speak*. Thus, if you refer to Atticus Finch as a *dumb ass*, then your thesis is really that Atticus Finch happens to have a rear end that is unable to speak with language. If that is your claim, then you are also in that category, Son. You also have a rear end that cannot use language." Mr. Looney is right next to Danny. Their noses are almost touching.

Danny is silent.

"Thus, to use your own theory, you, too, are a dumb ass." Mr. Looney smiles, his face still only inches from Danny's. "As am I. According to your definition, Danny, I am a dumb ass as well. And so are all of the students in this class."

Mr. Looney suddenly stands up straight, claps his hands, and says loudly, "Now that we've tackled that interesting idea, do you have any other thoughts you'd like to share with us, Daniel?"

I can't read Danny's face. I can't tell if he's going to leap out of his seat and punch Mr. Looney, or if he's going to run crying from the class. Maybe he's trying to decide himself.

"He should have just kept to himself—looked after his own stupid kids instead of trying to defend some black guy who was accused of rape. Trying to be some kind of stupid hero or something—" Danny catches himself, and I admit I'm shocked for the second time today: Danny's actually been reading the book. There's this wave of something going back and forth across his face.

"Daniel." Mr. Looney says his name and then is quiet for a long time. It feels like forever. He's just looking straight at Danny from across the room. Just looking at him. And for the longest time, Danny looks back too.

Then, finally, Danny looks down.

"Doing what's good is never about trying to be a hero; it's always about being exactly the person you are—the best version of who you really, really are." Mr. Looney pauses, then walks over to Danny again, and puts his hand on Danny's shoulder. "And anyone can do that, no matter what they're up against."

For a moment, the class feels like it's either going to explode or somebody is going to start laughing.

Instead, Danny brushes Mr. Looney's hand off his shoulder, looks up, and says, "Is the best version of you a teacher who pushes a high school student into a wall?"

And then I see Mr. Looney do something I've never seen before. I see him flinch. Like he's scared—like somebody hit him or something.

Danny stands up and his chair slides back with a screech. "Yeah, my mom found out all about it. You attacked one of your high school students, didn't you?"

My mind starts going crazy. *Is this true? Mr. Looney attacked a kid? Pushed him into a wall? What?!*

"You're not fooling anyone anymore, Looney Man. You crazy old geezer. My mom is going to take you down—you're done." Danny's voice has this razor in the middle of it, and it's weird to see the class change so suddenly, watching Danny mentally overpower Mr. Looney.

Walking away from Danny, Mr. Looney looks at the floor. He doesn't speak, and I wonder how many of my classmates are starting to believe Danny's story.

Finally, Mr. Looney turns and says to everyone, "It's true. Daniel is right about something."

"Ha! Told you! This old fart is gone—out of here." Danny starts walking toward the door as if everything is over. As if this crazy classroom experiment is finished.

"But Daniel is also very wrong about something." Mr. Looney takes a deep breath and sits down in his wooden chair. "The truth is that ten years ago I did push a high school student of mine into a wall. But the lie is in what Daniel failed to mention. The student whom I pushed was about to attack another student. What I did was my choice—but I did it because it needed to be done."

Danny, still by the door of the classroom with his back to Mr. Looney, turns and yells out, "Don't matter, Looney Man. After what you did to me today in class and what you did to that other student, you're still going down."

Then he opens the door and leaves the room, laughing.

When the door slams behind him, it's hard to tell if the wall that student was pushed into ten years ago isn't suddenly in this room, today.

I sit in bed that night with my back against the wall. I hold the copy of *To Kill a Mockingbird* that Mr. Looney let me borrow. I just stare at it. All I can think is that Danny must be wrong. There's no way Mr. Looney could have hurt a student.

I open the book to the title page, where Harper Lee's words to Mr. Looney—to *Robert*—about courage lie, complete with her autograph. After Mr. Looney first gave me the book, I did some searching online about Harper Lee. And what I found is crazy. She's still alive, but she's eighty-nine years old. That's even older than Mr. Looney. She grew up in this tiny town called Monroeville, Alabama, and her dad was a lawyer, just like Atticus Finch is in the book. A couple of Ms. Lee's friends thought she was an incredible writer, so they gave her enough money to quit her job as a secretary so she could try to write a book.

She thanked them and wrote the book *To Kill a Mocking-bird*. Everybody loved the book right away; it won prizes, and people started wanting to interview her, and they told her she was an amazing writer. But the really strange thing is that she kind of disappeared after that. She told people she didn't want to do any interviews, either. As far as anyone knows, she hasn't written anything else since, and right now she lives in the same tiny town where she grew up: Monroeville, Alabama.

On the Internet, I find out that *this* book I'm holding in my hands sold over forty million copies. FORTY MILLION COPIES. And then I find something even crazier. Before she wrote *To Kill a Mockingbird*, Harper Lee wrote another book called *Go Set a Watchman*. The publisher originally rejected that book, but they gave her suggestions on how to revise it. And then Harper Lee ended up using those suggestions to write the forty-million-plus bestseller. It's crazy. So I start wondering if *To Kill a Mockingbird* would ever even exist if the publisher hadn't asked for revisions and—kind of—rejected her first book.

As I'm sitting in bed, trying to think about what *forty million* really means, and how Harper Lee created a book that sold that much, I keep looking at her signature and her note to Mr. Looney. She must have known Mr. Looney really well. She doesn't talk to anyone about anything, but somehow she talked to Mr. Looney.

Who am I going to believe, then? A kid who beats me up and makes fun of me every chance he gets, or a teacher who earned the trust of Harper Lee and who—I can't deny it—has earned *my* trust?

But then again, why would Danny bring his mom into it unless it were true? Being on the school board, Danny's mom has some serious power, and she's not afraid to use it. She already had the hat policy changed at our school, and chances are if what Danny says about Mr. Looney *is* true—even in the smallest degree—then Mrs. Wills is going to do some serious damage.

I put my fingers across the word that Harper Lee wrote on the page: *courage*. I just let the tips of my fingers touch that word. Then I slowly drag them across the names *Robert* and *Harper Lee*.

When I finally turn to where I left off reading, I let my fingers touch the name of the dad in the book: *Atticus*.

TWENTY-FOUR

THINGS FALL APART

One morning, I walk into Mr. Looney's room early and find the lights off. No one's there. At first I think it's one of Mr. Looney's stunts—as if he is suddenly going to jump out from behind a bookshelf with some new surprise or idea to share with me.

"Hello?" I call out, walking slowly into the classroom.

No answer.

"Hello?" I try again.

Still nothing.

Crap, I think to myself. *Mr. Looney must be absent or running late.*

I decide to just stay and read like I normally do. I mean, the room is open, and Mr. Looney's old wooden chair is right there by his desk. He'll be in soon, I'm sure.

Setting down my backpack, I take out *To Kill a Mockingbird.* Last night I got to a pretty intense scene, and I only went to bed because my eyelids were closing on their own. So I'm psyched to get right back into the book this morning.

Atticus Finch, the father in the book, is just explaining to Jem and Scout (those are his kids) why he's doing what he's doing. Lots of the people in the town call Atticus names and threaten him for agreeing to be the lawyer for a black man accused of raping a white woman. Atticus doesn't think the man did it, but most people in town think he did, just because he's black.

I continue reading, flipping the pages like I used to do when I loved reading. I'm loving it again. I don't know how much time passes because the book gets really, really good. Jem keeps wanting his dad to be tough—to basically prove he's a *real* man. Finally, Atticus makes his son go visit this really, really old lady and read books to her. The old lady is pretty mean, but she's trying to stop using morphine before she dies. The morphine helps her not feel any pain from her disease.

So the old lady finally breaks free of being addicted to morphine. She dies with a lot of pain but with freedom and strength too. Jem asks his dad why he needed to watch the old lady do that, and what Atticus Finch says clicks inside of me like the words had been there all my life—just waiting to be released. Atticus tells his son Jem, "I wanted you to see what real courage was, instead of getting the idea that courage was a man with a gun in his hands. It's when you're licked before you begin, but you begin anyways. You rarely win, but sometimes you do."

I look up from the book.

Wow, I think.

Before we started the book, Mr. Looney gave us this big list of words we might not recognize. *Licked* was one of them. The whole class erupted in laughter at the word, but Mr. Looney assured us that *licked* didn't mean licking something with your tongue. Instead, he said, it meant *to be beaten*.

So, as I figure it, Atticus Finch is telling Jem that courage isn't about looking tough and having a gun—like all the guys do in the movies. Instead, courage is about doing what you think is right even if you think you'll lose. Even if you don't get any respect for it. Even if everyone laughs at you and thinks you're stupid.

As I'm sitting there in Mr. Looney's wooden chair, thinking through all this stuff, I hear the door to the classroom open and then quickly slam shut.

"Look who it is . . . it's Fatticus!"

How did he know I was in here . . . and why hasn't Mr. Looney shown up yet?

I feel a lump in my throat. I try hard to swallow, but the lump remains. I stand up from the wooden chair and slide it so that it is between me and Danny Wills.

"Oh—looks like Dwarf-boy is going to play hard to get, is he? Fine by me . . . it'll make it more fun." Danny approaches me, careful to remain right in my pathway to the door.

"Look, Danny, I was just finishing up reading . . . I've got to go to my locker before the bell rings." I feel myself lunging for words like one of them might be a shield to protect me.

Where are the words that will keep me safe? And where is Mr. Looney?

"All right, Fatticus, here are your choices: I can either give you a solid beating right here, right now, or you can drop your pants and give them to me." My chest tightens, and I can't breathe.

What would Atticus Finch do? I find myself wondering.

Then another part of me roars back at that thought. *Stupid question! Here you are about to get pulverized or humiliated, and you're wondering what a stupid made-up character would do? Who cares?! Run!*

But then the other part responds, *Wait a minute . . . what* would *Atticus Finch do? He said you've got to take a stand for what you know is right, even if you're going to get beaten. He said, you rarely win, but sometimes you do. It's just Atticus Finch and me right now, right here . . . just Atticus and me, and we've got to figure out what to do about the biggest jerk ever.*

Then, *Stupid, stupid, stupid! Run! Run! Run!*

I have to quiet the voices in my head, so I yell out loud, "Shut up!"

Danny's eyes shoot open even wider. "Oh, so you still think you're Mr. Tough Guy, do you? It's about time I chopped you down to your real size, Midget-man."

I see Danny lunge at me, and I slide the wooden chair in front of him. He falls flat on his face, and I hear a loud *smack* on the floor of the classroom. I rush to the classroom door. I'm just about to grab onto the handle—when I'm pulled backward by my shoulder.

I go down hard.

Danny's first kick lands on my right side, and I feel it burn into my skin. Before I can scramble away, I feel another kick to my head. My face feels raw and hot, and I bring my hand up to it. My jaw pulses with my heart. Then I feel my legs in Danny's hands, and he pulls me underneath a desk. Before I can figure out what he's doing, I feel the desk land hard on my back. I try to cry out as loud as I can, but my voice isn't there. My back throbs with heat, and I feel stinging running up and down my body. My head is dizzy.

Danny pulls the desk off of me and then he pulls a chair over so that it's right by my head.

I roll onto my back and look up through a thin slit in my eyes to see Danny holding the book Mr. Looney gave me.

"Oh, so Dwarf-boy gets his own special copy of the book, is that it? Let's just see what we've got here." Danny proceeds to rip the cover off of the book, tearing it into tiny pieces and dropping them on top of me.

"Whoops, did I rip that?" Danny's breaths are heavy. "Oh, wow, did you know that the author *personally* autographed this copy of the book? This must be worth a lot of money. That old bag of wrinkles must have asked her to sign this copy especially for him. It'd be a real shame to have it all destroyed."

Danny looks me dead in the eyes. He tears the autographed page from the front of the book, rips it into tiny pieces, then crushes them together in his hand.

"Whoops."

My eyes sting, everything aches, and the one object I care more about than anything else in the world has just been destroyed. And it isn't even mine.

Then things get worse.

Danny bends down and picks up a small, folded piece of paper from the ground. He opens it up and reads, "Dear Audrey, Your eyes are beautiful to me—" And then he erupts in laughter. "Are you kidding, Fatticus? *Really?!* This is hilarious . . . this is too funny . . . this is *beyond* funny. You think Audrey will go for a pint-sized portion of a midget like you?"

Danny holds the note above me, rips it into tiny pieces, and lets them rain down on me. They feel like stones, pelting my body.

Then the morning bell rings, and Danny runs.

⑥ ⑥ ⑥

Mr. Looney finds me on the floor, bloody and destroyed.

"Atticus . . . what happened?" He runs over to me and bends down beside me on the floor, his eyes wide and afraid.

But I'm so angry at him that I can't help shoving him away from me. Even though Danny ripped up his book—the book that was probably worth thousands of dollars—I still can't shake the feeling that Mr. Looney abandoned me. *Where was he when I needed him?*

Just like my dad.

Gone.

He knew I would be in his classroom early this morning, like every morning, but he decided not to show up. And I had to pay the price.

It was the same with my dad. He decides not to show up for our family anymore, and who has to pay the price?

Me.

And what help had Atticus Finch been to me? Did that stupid character keep the book from getting destroyed, my body from getting pummeled, my love note to Audrey from being shredded?

If this is how my life is going to be, then what's the point of trying to fight it? Why try to tell someone you love them? Why hope for something better and all of that crap? What does it really matter, anyway? Things don't change. Ever.

I slowly pick myself off the floor and walk clear out of the classroom and head out of the school.

In the hallways, kids stare at me like I've grown another head. They point at me with their mouths wide open. Mr. Looney walks alongside me the whole way, saying something to me. But I don't hear it.

I don't care what he's saying. The only thing I can hear in my mind, over and over, is this: *Things don't change.*

Ever.

TWENTY-FIVE

AUDREY HIGGINS & WHAT WORDS MEAN

I stay home from school for a week. I refuse to talk to anyone, even my little brother and my mom. I just don't know what to say anymore. I thought things were getting better. I thought my life was changing and things were finally going to start to work out for me.

Not the case.

Basically, I stay locked in my room the entire time except for when I have to use the bathroom or when a nurse comes over to change the bandages on my face and give me the once-over to make sure I'm healing.

I'm doing anything *but* healing.

A few times throughout the week, Mr. Looney stops by our house. My mom comes upstairs to my bedroom, saying stuff like, "Atticus, Mr. Looney is here and he really wants to talk with you about something. I think you need to hear what he has to say to you."

But I never go downstairs.

One time, I hear Mr. Looney's voice through the floor, saying something like, "He'll come when he's ready, just give the boy some time."

I don't know why, but I feel enraged to hear those words. If Mr. Looney had come when *he* was supposed to, Danny wouldn't have been able to do what he did.

Adrian tries knocking on my door a few times, asking if I want to watch stupid *The NeverEnding Story*. I almost yell something really mean at him, until I realize what's got to be running through his mind: I mean, here's this six-year-old kid who just wants to go around making farting noises and thinking that the world is a big, happy place, and now all of a sudden his dad leaves and his older brother comes home from school bloodied and gives everyone the silent treatment. So I don't yell, but I don't open the door either. I just can't deal with anyone right now, and I mean *anyone*.

Until my mom knocks and says the words that finally make me turn the lock and open the door.

"Atticus, Audrey Higgins is here."

For the first time in a week, I feel *almost* alive again. My heart starts beating fast, and my skin tingles just a bit. It seems now that somehow—miraculously—the arrival of Audrey Higgins has woken something up inside me.

But then, even as I start to leave my bedroom, the tingling leaves and the anger returns.

I walk down the stairs and into the living room, where Audrey sits on the couch with a glass of water. Her head goes back just a bit when she sees me. I know I look like a Halloween costume, with my pair of black eyes and dark red lines crisscrossing my face.

"Atticus, I'm so sorry about what happened to you." She slides over on the couch to make room for me, then pats a spot next to her. I can sense my mom watching us from the kitchen and, for a quick moment, I feel normal again.

But it passes, and I hear myself say to Audrey, "No thanks."

No thanks?! Atticus, what the heck are you doing? Audrey Higgins is right here in your living room, asking you to sit beside her on the couch! Have you lost your marbles?

My mind rages against me, but some other part of me is speaking, and I can't stop the words from coming out of my mouth.

"Why did you come over?" I hear myself ask Audrey, my voice flat.

"Because I was worried about you—I mean, you haven't been to school in a week. I wanted to see if you were okay." Audrey looks suddenly hurt, like *she's* the one who got pummeled instead of me.

"Oh," I say. "Well, have you seen enough?" Behind me, I hear my mom gasp. Adrian pokes his head out of the kitchen, but I don't even care if he hears this or not. He's been protected long enough. Maybe he should see what the world is really like. I don't care that my mom hears it either.

I just don't care.

Audrey stands up. "You know, Atticus, I think Danny is just as evil and awful as you do. But I didn't do this to you, and neither did Mr. Looney. We're on your side, you know that?" She looks away from me fast. I hear her breath catch.

But I feel even angrier now. "If you and Mr. Looney are both on my side, then where were you while Danny was pounding me, huh? Where was Mr. Looney then?"

My anger breaks loose, and I turn away from Audrey so that she can't see me starting to cry.

With my back to Audrey, I can't stop. Now that the words are coming, everything in me feels hot and explosive. I look at the ground and—

"When has anyone ever been there for me? Who can I trust? There's no one—and the people I think are *supposed* to be there leave me when I need them most. There's this whole world of people who just go on and on with their days, pretending like everything is totally fine, but inside, we're caving. Inside, we're crying. We want our fathers back. I *want* my father back. But he doesn't want me . . . he doesn't care about me at all. No one does."

Audrey puts her hand on my shoulder. One part of me wants to turn around and give her the biggest hug I've ever given another human being in my life. But the other part of me says she's just trying to be nice—that she doesn't *really* care. And she'll end up leaving too.

Neither part of me wins. So I wait.

Audrey lifts her hand from my shoulder, and then I hear something rustling. From the corner of my eye I can see that she's holding out an envelope to me. When I don't turn around and take it, she puts the envelope on the floor in front of my feet.

"Read that. You'll know that there *are* people who care about you. And you'll know where Mr. Looney was."

With that, Audrey turns around and leaves my living room.

TWENTY-SIX

THE LETTER

I grab the envelope off the floor then go back upstairs and lock the door to my room once more. I sit down on my bed and open the letter. This is what it says:

Dear Atticus,

You are at home right now thinking that I somehow left you in that classroom all alone on purpose. I can see you sitting in your room, your anger pouring out at me, at your family, at God, at the world for your situation in life right now. *It's not fair*, you're thinking, and you're absolutely right. It is, indeed, not fair that in this world there can be so much pain, so much hurt, so much wounding that we give and receive from one another. And nothing makes this hurt that we have to deal with fair. Nothing provides an excuse for it.

But you need to know something else, Atticus. You need to know that even with all of the difficult situations you have had to deal with so far, you are stronger. You are stronger than anything you have had to face. Atticus, I have seen your eyes light up as we talk about books and characters; I have seen ideas spread like wildfire through you, and I have heard you share some of the most moving and profound statements I have heard in all my years of teaching.

Atticus, I know that you don't see it in yourself, but you have a rare form of courage that you don't even realize. You do not have to be afraid of the courage you possess. It's okay to allow that courage into your life, to let it breathe through you, to feel it and to trust it and to follow it. Because, contrary to what everyone else tells you, and contrary to what I know you've seen in your own father and in the bullies at our school, courage is simply one thing. That's all: one thing.

Courage is the ability to keep going no matter how hard life feels. Courage is simply getting up each and every morning and saying, "I am not going to quit, no matter what happens." You can't always change the situations around you, but what you can always do is refuse to quit, refuse to say "I give up."

Remember when we talked about the iceberg in class? Surfaces tell us so little of what life actually means—so little of what has actually occurred. We, all too often, regard one another as icebergs—seeing only the top five percent and ignoring all that is deeper. Courage enables us to move forward, believing that, underneath the surface, joy and truth and beauty will emerge once more.

Thus, there's one other thing I want to tell you in this letter. That morning at school, the reason I wasn't in the classroom is that Principal Callahan stopped me on my way into the building. He summoned me to his office where a student's mother (who is also a member of the school board) was demanding to talk with me immediately. This mother told me that I had a vendetta against her son, and though I tried to reason with her, I fear we didn't make much progress. But because of this meeting, I arrived too late to help you.

I wanted you to know these things, though. Atticus, re-member that you are a young man of great courage. I see it in you, and I am proud of the person you are and the person you are becoming. No one can change the strength you have—and no one can tear down your courage unless you let them. They can tear all the paper in the world, but your courage is something they can't get at unless you hand it over to them.

Sincerely Yours,

Mr. Robert Looney

I hold the letter in my hands for a long time. I read it a second time. Then a third time.

Courage.

I think about what Mr. Looney has written, turning it around and around in my head. I fold the letter again and slip it into my back pocket. Then I rush down the stairs and out the back door of my house. There's somewhere I have to go.

At the sewer, I sit down inside the tunnel, right on the edge so that the light still touches me. I take the letter from my pocket and read it again.

Courage.

The word stings me. It makes me feel like I have a choice. That somehow, there's something I can do—some action I can take. I don't know exactly what that action is, or how to go about doing it, but Mr. Looney's words open up some possibility inside of me.

I look down the long tunnel toward the end. The lights are still there. I realize that my friends and I never got very far along inside of the tunnel when we were kids.

Every time we made our chalk marks, we would get a little farther. And we were always happy with the progress we'd made. We never *needed* to make it to the light at the end of the tunnel. It was enough for us to know that the light was *there*. And that light kept us going back to the tunnel as often as we could. The challenge of getting just a little closer every time was what it was all about.

Just to make a new chalk mark was enough. But then I started giving up on making chalk marks in my own life.

I take off my shoes and feel my feet sink right into that trickle of disgusting sewer water. I don't care. I just stand there letting that black water bubble up against my feet, and I close my eyes really tightly and try to remember. I try to remember me and Adam and my other friends starting down the tunnel, chalk in our hands, ready to get a little farther.

And finally, I feel it. My eyes burst open, and it's no longer sewer water gathering at my feet.

I'm ready to pick up some chalk and start walking again. It's time I made a new mark.

TWENTY-SEVEN

LITTLE BROTHERS SOMETIMES SPEAK THE TRUTH

When I get back home from the Tunnel to Heaven and Hell, there's a huge piece of green construction paper folded in half on my bed. I open it up to find a big photo of Adrian and me on a roller coaster ride called Venom. It's this monstrous roller coaster that does three upside-down loops and two jaw-dropping, ear-popping, gravity-defying descents.

Adrian and I went on the ride last summer, almost a year ago. He was terrified to do it, but I convinced him. I remember sitting on the bench in front of the ride telling him that I knew he could do it, that he would be fine, and afterward, we would both get popcorn balls and talk about how awesome it was.

Adrian had looked at me in horror, as though he were thinking, *How can I eat a popcorn ball if I'm dead?*

But somehow, my words hit home and he agreed to go on the ride. The entire time he screamed like I had never heard him scream in my life. Then, as soon as the ride stopped, the scream became laughter.

We bought the photo that they take during the ride, and in it I'm looking right at Adrian. My eyes are saying, *I love you, kid brother, and I'm proud that you came on this ride.* Adrian is hunched down into the seat of Venom's coaster, and his barely-open eyes are saying, *Don't let me die! Don't let me die! PLEASE don't let me die!*

As soon as we got home from that day at the amusement park, Adrian went proudly to his room and taped that picture of us to the wall right above his bed.

Now, that photo of us sits taped right in the middle of the green construction paper, and underneath, Adrian has written the words: ATTICUS & ME BEING BRAVE!

TWENTY-EIGHT

WHERE i COME FROM

Before going to bed, I decide to do something I've wanted to do for a long time: find out why my name is Atticus.

With everything that has happened with Danny Wills, and with my dad leaving, and now with Mr. Looney and Audrey, it's time I figured out why I've got a name that makes it so easy to torment me.

Even though *To Kill a Mockingbird* showed me something good about my name, I need to know why my parents gave it to me. I need to know that it wasn't some stupid joke they played on their first kid—or some bet with friends that they lost. You know: *All right, if you lose the bet, you've got to name that baby in your belly Atticus* [LAUGHTER ALL AROUND] . . . *Atticus!*

My mom is sitting at the kitchen table, a mug of tea in her right hand. No book in front of her—as I often found her before Dad left—and no newspaper or pad either. She's just sitting there, her eyes red and worn.

"You got a minute, Mom?" I stand by the kitchen table, a good distance away from her.

I don't want to commit to a long conversation—which is what I would be doing if I took a seat across from her at the table. On my feet, I feel safer. I can get away as soon as I want to if things get too emotional, or if the real origin of my name is something like: *Oh, I don't know, your father just thought it would be different.*

"Sure, honey . . . I've always got a minute. Take two, if you like." My mom used to say this all the time. It feels good to hear it again now.

"Well, it's just this question I have. A question I've *had* . . . for a long time, I mean."

I wait.

My mom waits.

Surprised that she doesn't just start asking a million questions, I take a deep breath and dive in.

"My name. Who named me?"

There. It's done. I've finally asked the stupid question that has been nagging me since I-can't-remember-when-it-wasn't-nagging-me.

"Your name? *Atticus*, you mean? Who named you?"

"Did Dad want me to be named Atticus? Was it his idea?" I brace myself.

But then something wonderful happens. First, my mom smiles. Then, she laughs just a little bit. Then, she tries to talk while she's laughing, and all that does is make her laugh even harder. So then she *really* starts laughing. "Did your dad [laughter] . . . *your dad* [more laughter] . . . *YOUR DAD* [uncontrollable laughter]?!"

It's hard to follow exactly what's going on in my mom's head. But she just keeps laughing, and soon her laughter pulls me in. I haven't seen my mom so happy in a long time, and some part of me wants to be in this happiness too—even if I'm not exactly sure what it's all about.

So there we are: my mom sitting at the kitchen table, me standing a few feet away from her, both of us laughing hysterically for different reasons, but laughing hysterically *together*.

And then Adrian comes down the stairs.

"Why is everybody laughing? It's bedtime! Why are you laughing?"

He comes over to me and starts hitting me on my arm, as if to demand, *Tell me what's so funny?!* I can't tell Adrian anything because I don't know myself. So instead, I do the only thing that occurs to me to enable my little fart-loving brother to laugh with us.

I fart.

It's a real fart, and it's a good one. Adrian loves it. My kid brother starts laughing immediately. And once the smell follows the sound, he laughs even harder.

Usually, my mom would frown on this kind of behavior, but tonight even she is loving it, and she just laughs even harder.

There we are: the Hobart family.

A husband and father left us, I got beat up (twice) pretty badly, my mom has been crying every night, and Adrian doesn't know what the heck is going on. But in the kitchen late that night, none of that matters.

The only thing that matters is that we're together.

I don't know how long it takes for all of us to finally calm down, but once we do, my mom motions for Adrian to come over to her. He does, and she picks him up and sits him on her lap. Then she tells me to come over to her too.

I do.

She pulls me in close to her, and she puts her arms around Adrian and me and squeezes us both really tightly. I feel safe.

"Your dad *hated* the name Atticus."

Now I'm sitting in the chair across from my mom, and Adrian remains on her lap. My kid brother seems to somehow get that what my mom is telling me is important, and—unusually for him—he doesn't interrupt.

"He begged and begged me to consider some other name. But I wouldn't. See, Atticus, when I was a young girl—about your age—I read the same book I see you reading every morning and every night, *To Kill a Mockingbird*. And as soon as I met Atticus Finch, I knew I had found the best thing about being human: courage. I knew I had found what it means to love other people even when it's hard and to fight for other people, even when it's hard."

My mom takes a deep breath then adds, "The opposite of my own father."

A thousand questions jump to my mind, but I let my mom finish.

"So, when I was thirteen, I decided that when I had my first baby boy, his name was going to be Atticus. I didn't care if the name was weird or if other people thought it was stupid or anything else. I just knew that with that kind of name, my son would grow up to be a strong and courageous young man. Your dad fought me and fought me on it, but I wouldn't budge. Something a person decides when they're thirteen years old and spends the rest of her life believing doesn't change all that easily. So, finally, he relented and let me name you. And right after you were born, I held you close to me—right up to my face—and I looked at you and I said, *I love you, my Atticus*. And you looked right back at me with those clear, bright eyes, and I knew you were saying *I love you* right back to me."

My mom looks at me then—I mean really *looks* at me. Her eyes soften, and she reaches across the table and touches my cheek.

"And I knew that you were going to grow up to be just as strong and courageous as Atticus Finch."

I look across the table at my mom and ask, "Am I?"

Her hand remains on my cheek and something rushes to her face. Water fills her eyes and she nods her head up and down. "You are. You are. You are."

TWENTY-NINE

GOING BACK

When I wake up the next morning, I know it's time. Even though I'm still scared, I know that I've got to go back to school.

In math class, Audrey moves her seat so that she's sitting next to me. She doesn't say anything, and even though Mrs. Relton sees her do it, Mrs. Relton doesn't say anything either. Danny sits in his normal seat and glares at me. This is what his eyes say: *I will eat you like a beef taco, Fatticus.*

I know that my face is still pretty bruised, but there's this thing inside of me that doesn't feel bruised at all. Instead, the inside-thing feels even stronger now than it ever did before. So I look into Danny's eyes, and I smile back at him. Then, I laugh just a little, because my Imagination kicks in and shows me Danny and a police officer:

Officer: [Chewing on a toothpick.] *Well, there . . . er . . . Danny. Looks like you think you're a tough guy, eh?*

Danny: *No . . . I mean, no, not really.* [Danny cowers in fear, does not look at Officer.]

Officer: *Let me tell you a little something, Danny. You see, I have this rule about bullies. Would you like to hear the rule I have about bullies?* [Officer takes toothpick out of his mouth and snaps it in half. The sound causes Danny to flinch.]

Danny: *Not really, Officer. No . . . I would not like to hear your rule . . . Please . . .* [Danny pushes his chair away from the interrogation table, looks around for help, but no one is there.]

Officer: *Good, I'm glad you want to hear my rule about bullies.* [Continues snapping toothpick into smaller and smaller pieces, then finally throws the pieces onto the floor and steps on them with his heavy black boot, grinding them into dust.]

Danny: *I said I didn't want to hear your rule . . . Officer, please, really, I'm sorry, please . . . just let me go.*

Officer: *All right there, Danny, I'll tell you the rule. I already said I would. No need to beg me. Here goes: my rule is that whatever a bully does to his victim, I do to the bully. Seems like a fair rule, doesn't it?* [Officer stands up and approaches Danny.]

Danny: [Hides his face in his hands, begins to cry.] *Please, Officer, I'm sorry . . . please, I won't ever do it again . . . please!*

Officer: [Stops and remains standing almost on top of Danny; reaches out his hand and makes a slow fist, each finger following the last, until his hand is curled tightly.] *Well, now, Danny, where would you like the first hit? I'd like to give you a little say in the matter, after all . . .*

Of course, since Danny is still sitting here in math class, I know these visions are completely impossible. The law won't be coming for Danny. And I'm not even sure that is what I *really* want—you know, deep down want. Don't get me wrong, I still hate Danny with a passion, but maybe there's another way to defeat someone like him. Maybe the way to win isn't in dishing back to him what he dishes out to me.

Mrs. Relton calls me to her desk. "Atticus, you've got a lot to catch up on. We covered coordinates and began plotting while you were absent . . ." As she speaks to me, she kind of looks away, as if it's too painful for *her* to see me so bruised and beaten. Then—almost like an afterthought—she looks right at me. "Look, Atticus. Don't worry too much about catching up, okay? Are you feeling all right?"

Mrs. Relton has never even tried to pretend that she liked me. Now, here she is, caring about me—and not pretending.

"Thanks, Mrs. Relton. I appreciate that." Her eyes are blue-gray and a little bit grainy, almost like a station on television that doesn't come in quite so good.

And then Mrs. Relton—of all people!—and I share this tiny moment. She's looking at me, I'm looking at her, and she says, "I hope everything is okay for you, Atticus . . . I really do. I hope you know that." And I know she means it.

I walk back to my seat. Audrey leans toward me, and as she comes closer, I feel this *heat* coming from her. Energy—like when a car's engine revs as it's climbing some massive hill. All this time Audrey's been revving some engine inside of her, climbing up these huge hills, and I've only ever seen myself.

But I'm not the only one facing a battle.

"Atticus, you need to hear what's happening. You need to know what's been going on here since you left. Meet me in the hallway." Audrey leans away from me then raises her hand. "May I please use the bathroom, Mrs. Relton?"

Mrs. Relton looks suspicious for a moment but then says, "Sure, Audrey."

I wait a few minutes—all the while knowing that *of course* Mrs. Relton is not going to let me use the bathroom. She has to know Audrey and I are going to talk.

I decide that it doesn't matter. "Mrs. Relton, can I use the bathroom?"

Her grainy eyes find me, she smiles, then says, "Of course, Atticus." I'm not kidding.

Audrey's waiting in a little alcove, a few doors down from Mrs. Relton's class.

"The library. And quickly." Audrey's hushed words give me no clue about what's going on and why she needs to talk to me immediately.

When we get to the library, we sneak into the nonfiction stack, toward the back, where no one ever goes anymore. Nowadays whenever there's any kind of research project, everyone races right to the computers. And it feels sad, suddenly, that these books are just sitting here, totally ignored.

But before I can think too much about the lives of nonfiction books, Audrey grabs my hand and yanks me to the floor. I lose my balance and actually fall back, knocking my head lightly on the bookshelf behind me.

"Sorry, Atticus." Audrey squeezes my hand hard. "Look, I'm glad you've decided to come back and all of that, but there's something pretty bad going on—and you need to do something about it."

Something bad?

And I need to do something about it?

"What do you mean? What's going on?" I feel lost for words, and yet somehow, that something is right. Something is very, *very* right.

"Something is wrong, Atticus. Something is very, *very* wrong." I swear her hand is going to squeeze my hand right off my arm.

"What's so wrong? I mean, Danny didn't pummel some other kid, did he?"

"No—worse than that." Audrey takes a short breath. "It's Mr. Looney."

I feel my body tighten; I think of the worst.

"Danny didn't kill him, did he?"

"No—Atticus, but it's bad. You know how Danny's mom is on the school board?" I nod, and Audrey continues.

"Well, Mrs. Wills is going to get Mr. Looney fired, maybe even in trouble with the police. Danny is saying that Mr. Looney was abusing him in class, taunting him, all kinds of garbage. It's like the Beena situation all over again. Except this time it's worse. It's bigger."

"But she can't really do that, can she? I mean, doesn't the whole school board have to agree and Principal Callahan and everything?" I can't figure out how one mother and son can inflict so much pain.

"Principal Callahan is tight with Mrs. Wills—seems like he'll do whatever she tells him to do. He already suspended Mr. Looney temporarily. And tonight the school board's having an open meeting to decide whether to fire him and then pursue a case against him in court for psychologically abusing Danny. Plus, Danny got tested by this psychiatrist, and his mom is holding up the results like a winning lottery ticket. They say Danny has signs of intense emotional abuse."

Audrey quickly takes a breath and adds, "Atticus, this is real. It's happening tonight, and Mr. Looney's job is on the line. Maybe even jail time. If Danny and his mom convince the school board that he abused Danny, they may be able to win their case—getting Mr. Looney fired *and* locking him up."

It *does* feel beyond belief. I thought the battle was over when I chose to return to school. After all, I made my decision not to give up. But this—this is bigger. I feel like there's nothing I can do.

"So—that's it, then? A guy finally comes and tries to help us see something that can change our lives, and now he's going to get fired and maybe even locked up?" It's not until the words are out of my mouth that I realize Mr. Looney wasn't ever the person I was angry at. He's the one who was *always* there for me. My dad is the one who left. Even though Danny found me alone in the classroom that morning when he beat me up, I wasn't really alone. Since Mr. Looney became my teacher, I've never been alone.

"Atticus, that's only what *might* happen. It doesn't have to be that way." Audrey looks at me, and I see that her brown eyes aren't only beautiful, they're strong. There's courage inside those eyes, enough to make the whole world different.

It doesn't have to be that way. I let her words dive inside of me. Because I want my eyes to say something like that too.

THiRTY

WHAT HAS BEEN TORN

Since we're already in the library, I ask Audrey for her help with what I know I've got to do.

"We have to find out where Mr. Looney lives," I say with a confidence that surprises even me.

"What do you mean?" Audrey looks at me, not understanding where I'm headed.

"I've got to see him before the meeting tonight."

Audrey nods her head, and we rush over to the computers, log in, and pray that at least one online address book isn't blocked by our school's filters.

Lucky for us, a URL goes through, and we come to a page where I type in *Robert Looney, Windsor, Connecticut*. And the next page reveals a phone number and an address. There's only one Robert Looney, so it's got to be him: 32 Wolcott Road, which is less than a mile from school. I know the street because it's where the baseball field is.

Crazy, I think. *While I was striking out, Mr. Looney was so close.*

"I've got to go. I'll stop by the office and call my mom; she'll understand—she'll sign me out of school for this. I've got to see Mr. Looney right now."

Audrey looks at me and nods, then touches my shoulder for just a moment. And then she's gone.

So am I.

The front door of 32 Wolcott Road is red. In the center of the door, there's a huge brass knocker, and I don't waste time before using it. Next to me on the porch are two wooden rocking chairs with a tiny white table in the middle of them. On the table is a book with a blue cover but no title on it. There's a pen lying across the top.

Some part of me wants to pick it up and read what's inside—*is it some kind of journal?*—and just when I feel like I can't resist seeing what's in there, the door opens wide to draw my eyes away from the book.

"Atticus. My, it's good to see you again." Mr. Looney stands large in the doorway, the light from inside the house coming out from all around him. His face looks somehow tired. Not like in English class.

Now that I'm here, I forget what I really want to ask, what I really want to say.

Mr. Looney takes the lead. "Come in, Son, by all means, please come in." He moves away from the doorway and stretches out his arm to welcome me inside.

The first things I see are the books.

The books!

This isn't a home; this is the downtown public library— but maybe the public library like I imagine it looked fifty years ago.

Books are piled high on tables. Books are stuffed into huge shelves that cover almost all of the walls in any direction that I look. There are books by the door, and there are books stacked next to the stairs.

And there's a book in Mr. Looney's hand.

He sees me looking at it and holds it up. "Actually, I was just thinking about you, Atticus, if you know what I mean." It's a copy of Harper Lee's *To Kill a Mockingbird*.

I smile. "Can I ask you something, Mr. Looney?"

"Of course, Atticus—anything." Mr. Looney leads me into the living room, clears away a stack of books from one of the chairs, and then motions for me to have a seat. He sits down opposite me.

"Why did you leave? I mean, did you try to fight Danny and his mom? Are you going to fight them? They can't do this to you. It's how Danny has always been, making other people's lives miserable and never being held responsible for it." I take a deep breath, surprised by how much comes pouring out of me so fast now that we're sitting.

Mr. Looney looks at me in a way my own father never did.

"Atticus, have I ever told you about my wife?"

"What? I mean, no. I didn't even know you were married. Is she here?"

Mr. Looney looks a little sad. "In a way, yes. She's always somewhat here. But she died in body a long time ago—ten years now."

"I'm sorry, Mr. Looney."

"Thank you, Atticus." He shifts his body and leans forward in his chair. "She was a writer, you know. Margaret Looney. She wrote many books—each one better than the one before, if I say so myself." He gets up, strides over to the bookshelf behind him, and grabs a book off of the shelf.

"This one is my personal favorite," he says and hands me the book. I read the title: *Finding Godot*. The cover is all black, except for the words, which are beige. The name *Margaret Looney* is on the bottom of the cover. The book is pretty thick.

"What's it about?" I ask.

"Well, first you need to know that there was another book written long before my wife wrote this one. It was called *Waiting for Godot*, and that book was about two men who do nothing but sit around and wait for a man named Godot to show up and meet them."

"What? There's a whole book about two guys waiting around for another guy to meet them? Who would ever want to read a book like that?" Even though I don't get how in the world some book about two guys waiting has anything to do with Mr. Looney being fired and maybe sent to jail, I know him well enough to guess that it's going somewhere.

"As it turns out, Atticus, many people would. And still do. While my wife admired the writing in that book, she told me one day that she wanted to rewrite it—make those guys do something other than sit around waiting. She believed that if all you do in life is wait, you'll never become who you were born to be."

Mr. Looney holds out his hand, and I give back the book. He stands up, exhales, and turns back toward the bookshelf.

"Atticus, I taught for many years, and I always hoped in some small way that I would teach until I left this world. The idea of retiring always felt strange to me. Why retire from something you love? For what? To sit around waiting to die?"

All my dad had ever talked about was how many more years he had to work until he could retire. I wonder if my dad had found a job he loved as much as Mr. Looney loves teaching—would it have made a difference? Could my dad still find a way to be happy?

"But after Margaret died, I stopped teaching. Nothing made sense, and I couldn't get out of bed to go see my students anymore. I had taught long enough to be able to retire, so I did. I left. I broke my own hope. And I spent a lot of years waiting. Just waiting to die, in a sense."

He turns and looks directly at me.

"And now?" I ask.

"This year, I decided to stop waiting. I came back when I saw that the school needed someone to cover a maternity leave. And I don't regret it at all."

"But what are you going to do *now*, Mr. Looney? What about Danny and his mom? What about the school board meeting? Audrey said they might even try to send you to jail."

Mr. Looney smiles at me like I just said something about a cruise in the Bahamas rather than him getting fired and maybe going to jail.

"Atticus, I'm still not interested in waiting. Lord knows Margaret would be furious with me if I said I'd just wait this one out." He places his wife's book back on the shelf. "I'll be at the school board meeting tonight, and I'll be ready to speak with passion and power. About that, there is no doubt."

I look at this teacher, *my* teacher. There's something else I need to tell him.

"I'm sorry about your book, Mr. Looney—the autographed copy of Harper Lee's *To Kill a Mockingbird*, I mean. I know it must have been worth a ton, and I know there's no way to replace it—"

Mr. Looney cuts me short. "Atticus, there's nothing torn that can't be repaired in some way or another."

I don't get it. There's no way the book can be replaced or repaired—I am sure of that. And I already know that the author, Harper Lee, is older than Mr. Looney. How would he ever find another original copy of the book and get her to write a note to him and autograph it again?

"I don't understand. How can it be replaced or repaired?" I ask.

Mr. Looney smiles at me. That smile that makes me feel safe.

"Atticus, it's not the autograph that's worth a lot, it's what the book means to you, and to me, that's worth a lot. And what the book means can't ever be torn unless you tear it yourself. Do you understand what I am telling you, Atticus?"

"You're talking about courage, aren't you?"

Mr. Looney doesn't answer. Suddenly, I know what I came here to learn—and what's more, I know what I need to do tonight at the school board meeting. So I stand up and thank Mr. Looney.

Just as I'm about to leave, I hear his voice. "Oh, before you go, Atticus, there is one more thing."

"What's that?" I ask.

"Here—you might need this."

He takes out a piece of paper from his shirt pocket. It's covered completely in tape. At first, I can't figure out what it is. So I walk toward him, and he holds it out to me. When I finally see it, I almost lose my balance. Mr. Looney's hand shoots out, and he grabs my arm to steady me.

Somehow, Mr. Looney managed to find *every single shred* of my love note to Audrey Higgins. Every piece is perfectly in place. It's like the note wasn't even ripped—just covered in a sheet of transparent tape.

When I reach out to take the note from him, Mr. Looney says, "Remember, Son, there's nothing that's been broken that can't be redeemed in some way. Nothing."

THIRTY-ONE

NIGHT

In the meeting room that night, the seven members of the school board sit on a raised platform. It's worse than I thought, because Mrs. Wills has this little place card in front of her that reads "Susan Wills, School Board Chair." She sits right in the middle of the seven. Like Danny *during* school, she's got the power here *after* school.

My mom is with me. I told her I wanted to come alone, but she wasn't about to let that happen. "You go, I go, Atticus," she said.

We take two of the maroon plastic chairs toward the back of the room and watch the other people come in. I'm surprised to see all kinds of people: some other students from my English class, lots of parents, and even some really old people.

None of the board members look like they're in a very good mood. Mrs. Wills, especially, looks like she wants revenge.

The room is packed. By seven o' clock, some people are even standing on the sides and in the back of the room. Only a couple handfuls of scattered seats are still empty. Still no sign of Mr. Looney, though. But there's plenty of Danny Wills. He's easy to see, off to the side of the platform, and in his eyes I see the (all-too-fake) look of a hurt student. He's putting on his best stuff, trying to play the part of an abused student.

I'm disgusted by Danny—even more than I've ever been before, and that's saying a lot. But just as I'm about to look away, I catch something out of the corner of my eye: Danny's father. I haven't seen him since my last baseball game. He's looking at Danny and shaking his head, saying something to his son.

Mrs. Wills comes off her seat on the stage and says something to her husband with a scowl on her face. Then Mr. Wills walks away from them both.

This tiny voice inside of me wonders, *What if?* I think back to the baseball game and what Danny's dad said to him—*get your butt over here*—and a question that I don't want to care about is waiting in my head: *What if Danny is an abused student, but not by Mr. Looney?*

Interrupting my thoughts, I hear the firm, angry voice of Mrs. Wills call everyone's attention.

"This meeting will now begin." Mrs. Wills pounds a gavel on the table in front of her, and I feel my heart speed up.

"There are a few items on the agenda for business tonight, but I'd like to begin with the likely reason for this outpouring of support from citizens, teachers, and students alike: the danger of Robert Looney within our school walls." She pauses.

I can see right away that the rest of the board is at least a little afraid of her. And I'm sure it doesn't help that they've probably heard of all the crazy things Mr. Looney did in our class. It wouldn't be a stretch to make the case that the guy *is* crazy. I even wondered that when I first met him, after all.

Mrs. Wills continues. "First, I'd like to read the list of grievances against said teacher, compiled from students—like my son, Danny, who was emotionally abused at his hands—and from teachers, from parents, and even from our principal, Mr. Callahan himself." At this mention, she pauses again and nods to recognize Principal Callahan in the front row of the hall.

"I'll begin by reading the three separate grievances, along with their descriptive proofs. Finally, I will read the committee's recommendation for Robert Looney. The committee that constructed these grievances and their correlating recommendations was composed of four members: Principal Callahan and three members of the school board, one being myself. In the process of our committee work, we met with all individuals having direct insight into this situation and with all those who would be directly affected by our decisions tonight."

Even though I hate Mrs. Wills right now, I'm a little amazed by her ability to use words to trick those who hear them. Danny—I figure—isn't far behind his mother.

While Mrs. Wills shuffles her papers and adjusts the microphone close to her mouth, I wonder which "individuals" the committee interviewed. No one asked me. No one asked Audrey. I'm starting to see how the world can sometimes make anything seem true even if it's not proven. That's exactly what it must have felt like for Atticus Finch.

And still he made his case.

There's a whisper behind me. "Hey, I'm here too. Sam's with me and Margaret. Even Hannah came." It's Audrey. She must have shuffled in just now and found a way to sit near me. Sam is next to her and the others she mentioned: more Looney supporters.

Mrs. Wills clears her throat and begins. "Grievance number one: Creating an unsafe learning environment. Robert Looney has engaged in reckless classroom behavior, including wearing inappropriate attire, yelling extremely loudly, and shouting words in other languages at the students in anger. He has cursed at students—including my son—and he has even made physical contact with students. This is no surprise,

193

considering his physical attack of a high school student in his own class, ten years prior."

Bodies shift all across the hall, and there's a hum of low voices—whether in approval or outrage, I can't tell.

"Grievance number two: Conducting no actual teaching. Robert Looney has not taught the students any of the provided state frameworks, nor has he even used paper in the classroom. Students have not been required to take a single test in the entire two months that Robert Looney has been their teacher."

Mrs. Wills takes a deep breath and shakes her head, as if disgusted by what she's reading.

"Grievance number three: Causing undue and intense emotional and psychological strain and stress and even— in some cases, as with my son, Danny—abuse through his strange methods and genuine dislike of certain students. Robert Looney has ridiculed specific students, calling them names and even making threats." There's audible gasping in the audience.

"Recommendations: while Robert Looney has already been suspended by executive decision of Principal Callahan, we feel that such a measure is not strong enough, considering the grievances against him. The committee moves to immediately formalize the termination of his position, to pass a statute that would bar him from ever working in this district again, and to consider further action against said teacher in a civil court."

Mrs. Wills puts down the papers and leans back in her chair, looking up at the crowd around her as if to ask, *Is there really any argument? We all know the guy is a psycho and should be as far away from our kids as possible.*

"The floor is now open for comment." I know Mrs. Wills hopes there'll be no comments—that the measures will pass quickly so that they can get Mr. Looney out of their sight for good.

As if on cue, Mr. Looney rises up from the dead middle of the hall. I don't know why I never noticed before how tall he is: the guy looks like a giant among a bunch of ants. The more I watch him, the more I feel myself relax. Even my worry about speaking fades. My body feels still.

The room is silent, waiting.

When Mr. Looney speaks, his voice booms. It's as if my chair vibrates beneath me.

"When I was a young man—just leaving boyhood—my father gave me a poem that he had copied from a small book. It was a short poem, and he left it by my bedside one night, so that I found it the next morning when I awoke." Mr. Looney pauses.

"I made it my goal then to try to live my life by the message of that poem. Now, as an old man, all I have left is the hope that I have honored the dream of a young man—and the message of a great poet." He clears his throat and then continues. "Robert Frost once wrote:

> Two roads diverged in a yellow wood,
> And sorry I could not travel both
> And be one traveler, long I stood
> And looked down one as far as I could
> To where it bent in the undergrowth;
>
> Then took the other, as just as fair,
> And having perhaps the better claim,
> Because it was grassy and wanted wear;
> Though as for that the passing there
> Had worn them really about the same,
>
> And both that morning equally lay
> In leaves no step had trodden black.
> Oh, I kept the first for another day!
> Yet knowing how way leads on to way,
> I doubted if I should ever come back.

I shall be telling this with a sigh
Somewhere ages and ages hence:
Two roads diverged in a wood, and I—
I took the one less traveled by,
And that has made all the difference."

I can't believe it.

Robert Frost.

Is it my Imagination again? Am I creating some sort of crazy vision where Robert Frost comes to save me at the last minute? Where—

Wait.

No.

This time, it's not about saving *me*. It's not about me at all. It's about something bigger than me.

My Imagination is quiet, and what's Real stands before me: silver hair, bushy eyebrows, green eyes that flicker like fire.

Mr. Looney speaks again. "And that is the truth—the beautiful, crazy, and *only* truth. Whether I have succeeded in my own dream will not be decided by you, Mrs. Wills, or by you, Principal Callahan. The outcome of this meeting will not change the poet's words, nor will it change my own heart. And it will especially not change the way I have tried to combine the two." Then his voice becomes really low, and he looks right at me. "Truth never exists where people's voices are not heard."

For a few moments, the room is tense and still. No one moves.

"Well, now that we've dealt with that—are there any other comments before we move to a vote?" Mrs. Wills' high-pitched, angry voice filling the room could not be more different than what I just heard.

I feel my skin tingle. The air around me is warm. But I don't raise my hand, and I don't stand up.

"All right then, we'll move to a direct vote by the board, and then we'll follow that with—"

"I have something to say." As I stand, my body shakes. My legs almost collapse under me.

I feel Audrey's energy behind me, and I hear her whisper, *Say it, Atticus; say it all.*

"What? Who said that? Where are you?" Mrs. Wills looks around the room, but she can't see me. Most people probably can't. Since I'm shorter than most thirteen-year-old kids, I don't rise above the crowd like Mr. Looney just did. Not even close to it.

"I'm speaking. Over here. I'm Atticus Hobart, a student of Mr. Looney's." As I say these words, I step onto my chair. Suddenly, I'm a giant. I'm looking down on everyone else around me.

And my legs are no longer shaking.

"Well, give your comments already, then," Mrs. Wills barks. "And please *be brief.*" She sits back in her chair and crosses her arms, as if to say: *You've got nothing, kid. You're beat—you and your crazy English teacher.*

I look over at Danny, and decide to begin with what was almost the end.

"I was recently beaten up badly by Danny Wills." I point directly at him. "I still have the scars on my face and body to show for it." I turn and look around the room. "I was beaten because I was in Mr. Looney's room early one morning, reading. So my crime, according to Danny, was reading." I stop and let these words sink in.

Mrs. Wills leaps to her feet and yells out, "My son is *not* on trial here! This reprobate of a teacher is!"

But her voice feels like nothing to me, and I keep on going. "I stayed home from school for a week—feeling sorry for myself, thinking that no matter what, I was never going to win at anything. I'd always be made fun of no matter what

I said or did." I look over at Mr. Looney. "But then I remembered what Mr. Looney taught me—what he tried to teach all of us, even Danny: that you don't have to win something to be respected; you just have to fight for what you know to be true—for what you really believe.

"For a while, I wanted to get revenge on Danny. And when I heard what you all were trying to do to Mr. Looney, I wanted to get revenge on all of you too—especially you, Mrs. Wills." I look right at her. She acts as though I'm about to attack her right then and there. "But I realize now that I don't want revenge. What I want is to be heard—for my voice to matter. That's all. Mr. Looney showed me that I count.

"All of that stuff you read just now is false, Mrs. Wills. School board members, I was in Mr. Looney's class. He never disciplined Danny—not once. He welcomed him into whatever we were doing and left him alone if he wouldn't join in. Danny knows it too, whatever is making him deny it. But he knows the truth.

"Mr. Looney's only crime is inspiring me and inspiring a lot of us." I look at Audrey and Sam and the others behind me. "Your decision tonight can't change what Mr. Looney taught all of us, and it can't take away the courage he's helped me find."

For the first time in a long, long time, I feel like—*me.*

"So you want to talk about *grievances*? I'll give you three real ones. Number one: Adults who do not take the time to listen to students or to believe them. Number two: People who keep all the power because they can and just make others miserable. Number three: Lying because you're afraid of the truth. It's about time to let some voices be heard that have been silent for way too long."

I look down at my mom, and she's wiping her eyes with her shirt sleeves, her hair, napkins—she's grabbing anything she can find to stop her tears.

When I sit back down, she says to me, "I am so proud of you." Then she hugs me really, really tightly. And I honestly don't care that I'm a thirteen-year-old being bear-hugged by a hysterically weeping mom.

THIRTY-TWO

KISSING & COURAGE

I'd like to write that after my speech, *everyone else* starts crying too. I'd like to write that the entire audience is overcome by the truth of my words, and everyone starts spontaneously chanting *Free Mr. Looney!* and *Mr. Looney for Principal!* and everything like that. I'd like to write that people applaud for me and carry me away from that school board meeting on their shoulders.

Instead, Mr. Looney is voted out by the school board. He's fired immediately by a vote of six members in favor, one opposed. This guy named Mr. Daniels gives a short speech after mine, saying you can't make up words with the kind of power mine have, so he supports Mr. Looney.

The school board does *not*, however, recommend any sort of civil action against Mr. Looney. On that count, Mrs. Wills is the only vote in favor.

Principal Callahan—of course—remains at his post, and I'll see him first thing tomorrow, I'm sure, introducing a new English teacher. Chances are it'll be someone normal. But that's okay: I know who I am now, and it feels so good to use my voice. I decide I'm going to start to make a habit of it in *every* one of my classes.

Before my mom and I drive off, Audrey tells me she's looking forward to seeing me at school. She also tells me that I've got a lot of courage for saying what I said.

Mr. Looney comes over to my mom and says, "Well, ma'am, it's lovely to make your acquaintance once more." He looks at me and winks. "I don't have to tell you that you've got one fine boy here. One *remarkable* son."

My mom smiles and nods her head, then puts her hand on my back. "You're right about that, Mr. Looney. My Atticus is something else, isn't he?"

In the weeks after the school board meeting, I feel different—but more myself too. I watch *The NeverEnding Story* with Adrian again (for the five hundredth time), and I even make farting noises with him when he wants me to. We have all kinds of competitions: who can fart the loudest, who can fart the longest, who can make the highest-pitched farting noise, who can make the lowest farting noise . . .

Danny ends up serving a week-long suspension, along with a discussion with a police officer (though probably not the way I imagined it). As it turns out, even if you claim a teacher is emotionally abusing you, you still don't have the right to pummel another kid. Mostly, he leaves me alone at school. I hang out with Sam a lot, and my voice comes out a lot more than it ever did before. If Danny tries to say stuff to me, my heart pumps and I tell him I don't want to hear it. I realize, now, that there are teachers who care too. "Fatticus" may still come from Danny once in a while, but he's never touched me again.

My dad comes to visit Adrian and me a few days after the school board meeting. He talks with us for a while, and he doesn't even ask about baseball. He listens when I tell him about the meeting, and he even kind of smiles when I get to the part where I stand up on the chair. It's not like he's Dad of the Year or anything, but I kind of feel like maybe there's a chance for something to happen. Maybe things can still have a chance to change.

My mom is pretty happy to see me going to school again, and to be honest, I'm pretty happy to be back at school. I gave Audrey my note the day after the school board meeting—Tuesday. This time, I didn't want to take any chances. I didn't want to *wait*.

In the middle of lunch, Audrey read it to herself and then stood up and yelled, really loudly, "YES!" And I'm not kidding about this next part.

Audrey came around to my side of the lunch table and planted one right on me. I mean, she gave me this big wet kiss when I wasn't expecting anything like it. Everyone in the cafeteria looked straight at Audrey and me. Whispers everywhere at first, then some hoots and hollers, and then finally, some kids started shouting, "Go, Atticus" and "All right, Audrey!"

To this day, I've never hit a home run (or even gotten a base hit, for that matter), but I had my moment at the school board meeting, and I had my moment in the cafeteria with Audrey. I know that I'm making chalk marks along the tunnel again.

And maybe that's what courage is all about.

Which brings me to a question: Why did I decide to write all of this down in a book anyway? Ever since that day when I heard Mr. Looney and Audrey talking at the end of class about why an author writes a book, I've been trying to find out what the answer is.

After TONS of pleading, Audrey finally caved and told me what Mr. Looney said: It's about believing that when you tell the story that only *you* can tell, you show other people that they're not alone, that all of us share some things, like fear, hope, and love.

That's kind of what Harper Lee showed me through Atticus Finch.

So I figured I would try it myself. Maybe I've got a story worth telling.

ACKNOWLEDGMENTS

This book only exists because of a lot of people who continued to believe in the story of Atticus and Mr. Looney with incredible resilience. I owe mountains upon mountains of thanks to my agent, Ammi-Joan Paquette, whom I first met at the Rutgers One-on-One Writing Conference. At every step of the process—from revisions of multiple drafts, to true re-envisioning of the entire manuscript for various submissions rounds—Joan was steadfast. This deep belief—coupled with remarkable knowledge and wisdom—helped make this novel what it is, and allowed it to meet the world. Joan: thank you so much for working tirelessly and believing with such depth of commitment. You rock. And thank you for the thousand other ways you encourage and support me and all of your writers. You seem to possess an unshakeable amount of faith, positivity, intelligence, and sense of humor—and these all shine in the way you work with stories and with people.

Jacque Alberta, at Blink YA, you are a wonderfully warm and wise editor and human being. When Joan called to tell me that the book would be in your hands, I cried and whooped and relished the opportunity. Working with you has been a delight, and I am thankful for the revisions, ideas, and arc you brought to Atticus. Thank you so very much! And to the rest of the BLINK YA team who have shown such kindness and support of the novel, including Liane Worthington, Sara Merritt, Sara Bierling, and others behind the scenes who I do not know but who have had a hand in this process. Thank you!

A writer I admire with all my heart, Kathryn Erskine, offered such encouraging correspondence, sharing warmth, kindness, and generosity far beyond the norm. She truly embodies the spirit of the children's writing community—and she even read and commented on an earlier draft of the novel, which lent both heart and hope to the endeavor. The novel's title is even her idea! With deep gratitude and respect, I am in awe of the energy you have, Kathy — your incredible talent and work ethic, and your generosity of soul and mind. Thank you.

To my fabulously funny, warmly weird, and perpetually loving dad, mom, and four brothers. Harry and Kathy Reynolds are big believers in dreams, who encouraged all of us to keep growing, thinking, wondering, and waiting in the pursuit of something beautiful and bold. Chris, Mike, Bryan, and Matthew: you fine gentlemen remind me constantly that deep, serious conversations and giddy, wild laughter are both important parts of togetherness, learning, and growth.

Mandy, Caleb, and Evan Reynolds, Harold Fenton, Susan and Wendell Anderson, David Anderson, Paul and Diana Gant, Wade Austin, Matthew Bednarz, Tamara Ellis Smith, Francisco Stork, Mike Jung, Olugbemisola Rhuday-Perkovich, John Dufresne, Jordan Sonnenblick—each of you showed genuine kindness and encouragement in varied ways, and your voices and ideas and examples were so essential to me and to this story. Thank you.

John Robinson and Robert Looney, to whom this book is dedicated in part, are the two teachers who most deeply personify what it means to be fully alive to writing, reading, and the power of words to change oneself and the world. You each awoke in me the power of story, and I owe to you each a debt of gratitude the likes of which I can only repay by telling stories— forever and ever and ever ...

And to Jennifer. Jennifer! We made it many long years wondering if such a pursuit was crazy. Yet you never wavered in your support, and in your belief in Atticus and his story. On illogical adventures across the Atlantic, when we were carless and soaked from cold rain and had bills to pay that could not be paid, you helped our family dance in the living room. On days when I felt no amount of revision or submission or hope was ever going to translate into action, you reminded me that I'd see it differently tomorrow. And on our tea walks and long, late-night talks, you shared your dreams, listened to mine, and together we imagined what could be. Thank you for all of it. Thank you for then, and thank you for now. Thank you for being my AUDREY HIGGINS.

Tyler and Benjamin: as you grow into bigger boys and then, one day, men, I hope that this story speaks to your hearts. I hope that you let Atticus live into your own lives, and that you see that real courage involves the way we love others even when no one else does or will. I love you both so much, and I am humbled and honored (and pretty giddy, too) to be your daddy.